Collins

Japanese

phrasebook

Consultant
Miyoko Yamashita

First published 2007
Copyright © HarperCollins Publishers
Reprint 10 9 8 7 6 5 4 3 2 1
Typeset by Davidson Pre-Press, Glasgow
Printed in Malaysia by Imago

www.collins.co.uk

ISBN 13 978-0-00-724679-3
ISBN 10 0-00-724679-X

Using your phrasebook

Your *Collins Gem Phrasebook* is designed to help you locate the exact phrase you need, when you need it, whether on holiday or for business. If you want to adapt the phrases, you can easily see where to substitute your own words using the dictionary section, and the clear, full-colour layout gives you direct access to the different topics.

The Gem Phrasebook includes:

- Over 70 topics arranged thematically. Each phrase is accompanied by a simple pronunciation guide which eliminates any problems pronouncing foreign words.

- A top ten tips section to safeguard against any cultural faux pas, giving essential dos and don'ts for situations involving local customs or etiquette.

- Practical hints to make your stay trouble free, showing you where to go and what to do when dealing with everyday matters such as travel or hotels and offering valuable tourist information.

- Face to face sections so that you understand what is being said to you. These example mini-dialogues give you a good idea of what to expect from a real conversation.

- Common announcements and messages you may hear, ensuring that you never miss the important information you need to know when out and about.

- A clearly laid-out dictionary means you will never be stuck for words.

- A basic grammar section which will enable you to build on your phrases.

- A list of public holidays to avoid being caught out by unexpected opening and closing hours, and to make sure you don't miss the celebrations!

It's worth spending time before you embark on your travels just looking through the topics to see what is covered and becoming familiar with what might be said to you.

Whatever the situation, your *Gem Phrasebook* is sure to help!

Contents

Using your phrasebook 3

Pronouncing Japanese 7

Top ten tips 11

Talking to people 13
Hello/goodbye, yes/no 13
Key phrases 15
Work 19
Weather 20

Getting around 22
Asking the way 22
Bus and coach 25
Metro 28
Train 30
Taxi 34
Boat and ferry 36
Air travel 38
Customs control 40

Driving 42
Car hire 42
Driving 44
Petrol 45
Breakdown 46
Car parts 47
Road signs 49

Staying somewhere 51
Hotel (booking) 51
Hotel desk 54
Camping 55
Self-catering 57

Shopping 58
Shopping phrases 58
Shops 60
Food (general) 61
Food (fruit and veg) 62
Clothes 64
Clothes (articles) 66
Maps and guides 67
Post office 68
Photos 69

Leisure 70
Sightseeing and tourist office 70
Entertainment 71
Leisure/interests 72
Music 72
Cinema 73
Theatre/opera 74
Television 76
Sport 77
Skiing 79

Walking	81
Communications	82
Telephone and mobile	82
Text messaging	86
E-mail	86
Internet	88
Fax	89
Practicalities	90
Money	90
Paying	92
Luggage	94
Repairs	95
Laundry	96
Complaints	97
Problems	98
Emergencies	100
Health	103
Pharmacy	103
Body	104
Doctor	105
Dentist	107

Different types of travellers	109
Disabled travellers	109
With kids	110
Reference	112
Measurements and quantities	112
Numbers	115
Days and months	117
Time	120
Time phrases	122
Eating out	123
Food in Japan	123
Reading the menu	130
Vegetarian	146
Wines and spirits	150
Grammar	151
Public holidays	160
Signs and notices	162
Dictionary	
English – Japanese	172

Pronouncing Japanese

Although the Japanese writing system is rather complicated, pronouncing Japanese is easy once you know the few basic rules. This book has been designed so that as you read the pronunciation of the phrases, you can follow the Japanese. This will help you to recognize the different sounds and give you a feeling for the rhythm of the language. A few rules for you to note are below.

In Japanese the basic unit of speech is the syllable, not the letter. Each syllable is pronounced approximately the same length and rather flatly. Japanese has a pitched accent (high and low) but tone doesn't change the meaning, as it does in Chinese. It is more important not to stress any one part of a word. For example, in English the word Paris is pronounced **pa**ris and in French pa**ree**. Japanese gives equal strength to both syllables: **pa**ri.

Japanese has relatively few sounds. Each vowel has only one sound.

Japanese vowels

	sounds like		
a	'a'	as in	bath
i	'i'	as in	police
u	'u'	as in	put
e	'e'	as in	let
o	'o'	as in	got

Long vowel sounds

aa, ii, uu, ee, oo   approximately double the
length of other syllables

15 Basic consonants

k, s, t, n, h, m, y, r, w, g, z, d, b, p, n/m

Except **n/m**, and **shi**, **chi** and **tsu**, a consonant
takes one vowel to create a syllable as in
Ki-mo-no   traditional Japanese costume
Ta-na-ka   Japanese surname

These consonants are close to their English
equivalents but note the following:
g is pronounced as in **g**olf, not as in **G**ermany
y is pronounced as in **y**oung, not as in cr**y**

Since Japanese lacks the consonants **l** and **v**, foreign loanwords with these letters are pronounced with **r** and **b**, respectively. Thus, English words 'love' and 'rub' both become indistinguishable as **ra-bu** in Japanese.

Japanese also lacks the **si** sound (as in 'to sit'): **shi** is used instead, with often embarrassing results! Other English sounds that do not exist in Japanese are **hu** (as in 'hook': **fu** is used instead); **th** (as in 'thin': **shi** is used instead); and **ti** (as in 'tin': **chi** is used instead).

Double consonants, like **kk**, **pp**, **ss** and **tt** are written before a vowel, which indicates a pause equivalent to one syllable in length before that consonant. The sound before the pause tends to become sharper than at other times.

	Pronunciation	Meaning
kitte	ki (pause) te	stamp
kippu	ki (pause) pu	ticket

ki, **shi**, **chi**, **ni** ,**hi**, **mi**, **ri**, **gi**, **ji**, **bi** and **pi** sounds can be combined with **ya**, **yu** or **yo** to create combined consonants. For example, **ki** + **ya** become **kya**, **ki** + **yu** become **kyu** and **ki** + **yo** become **kyo**. Examples of this can be found in the words **Tookyoo** and **Kyooto**, where it is pronounced as two sounds, but said very quickly with the same length of one syllable.

	Pronunciation	Meaning
matchi	ma (pause) chi	match

In the case of the **chi** syllable, a double consonant sound is written as **tchi** as in the example above.

You should also remember that Japanese does not have a silent **e** at the end of a word such as in the English 'to take'. If 'take' is read as the Japanese word **take** (bamboo), it should be pronounced tah-keh. Similarly **sake** (rice wine), is pronounced sah-keh, etc.

However, the vowel **u** at the end of a sentence such as **Mike desu** will sound very weak.

Top ten tips

....

1. Always remember to remove your shoes before entering someone's home. Before stepping on **tatami** matting, slippers must also be removed. Slippers must be changed when going to the toilet. Remember not to leave the toilet still wearing the toilet slippers, as it would be very embarrassing!

2. Always make sure that you do not have any holes in your socks or tights, as you may have to take your shoes off unexpectedly.

3. Shaking hands is uncommon in Japan; the Japanese greet each other by bowing. However, foreigners are sometimes greeted with a handshake.

4. **Sumimasen** is a word with many purposes: it can be used to attract someone's attention before making a request, or to get past people on a crowded train. It can also be used to say "sorry".

5 Credit cards are only accepted in the more expensive hotels, shops and restaurants.

6 If you receive a gift from a Japanese visitor, remember to express delight at the wrapping as well as the gift itself. If you are invited to a Japanese person's house, make sure you take gift-wrapped present with you.

7 You can only buy cigarettes and alcohol if you are over 20 years of age.

8 The Japanese tend not to use assertive words such as "yes" and "no". Good alternatives are **ii desu ne** for "yes" and **chotto** for "no".

9 Cleanliness is important to the Japanese. Never drop or leave rubbish.

10 It's advisable that you carry proof of identity at all times, so make sure that you always have your passport with you.

Talking to people

Hello/goodbye, yes/no

In Japanese there is no exact equivalent for the word 'hello' – different greeting words are used based on the time of the day. Similarly, the word **chotto** (whose literal meaning is 'a bit') is influenced by body language: if said with one's head slightly tilted, it means 'no'.

Hello	こんにちは
	konnichiwa
Good morning	おはようございます
	ohayoo gozaimasu
Good evening	こんばんは
	kombanwa
Good night	おやすみなさい
	oyasuminasai
Goodbye	さようなら
	sayoonara
See you later	じゃまた
	ja mata

See you tomorrow	また明日	
	mata ashita	
How are you?	お元気ですか	
	ogenki desu ka?	
Fine, thanks	はい、元気です	
	hai, genki desu	
And you?	あなたは?	
	anata wa?	
Please	お願いします	
	onegaishimasu	
Thank you	ありがとう (ございます)	
	arigatoo (gozaimasu)	
You're welcome	どういたしまして	
	dooitashimashite	
Excuse me!	ごめんなさい!	
	gomennasai!	
Sorry!	すみません!	
	sumimasen!	
Yes	はい	
	hai	
No	いいえ	
	iie	
Um...	ちょっと...	
	chotto...	
Yes, please	はい、お願いします	
	hai, onegai shimasu	
No, thanks	いいえ、結構です	
	iie, kekkoo desu	

Sir...	...氏
	...shi
Mr.../Madam.../	...さん
Mrs.../Ms.../	...san
Miss...	
I don't	わかりません
understand	wakarimasen
I don't speak	私は日本語が話せません
Japanese	watashi wa nihongo ga
	hanasemasen

Key phrases

••••••••••••••••••••••••••••••••••

There is no gender, article or singular/plural form in Japanese. Different counters are used together with numbers (please see the number section for more detail).

museum	美術館
	bijutsukan
the station	駅
	eki
the shops	店
	mise
the houses	家
	ie/uchi

a/one	一つ
	hitotsu
a ticket	チケット一枚
	chiketto ichimai
one stamp	切手一枚
	kitte ichimai
a room	一部屋
	hito heya
one bottle	一本
	ippon
some (countable)	いくつか
	ikutsuka
some	いくらか
(uncountable)	ikuraka
some wine	ワインいくらか
	wain ikuraka
some fruit	フルーツいくつか
	furuutsu ikutsuka
some biscuits	ビスケットいくつか
	bisuketto ikutsuka
Do you have...?	...はありますか
	...wa arimasu ka?
Do you have a timetable?	時刻表はありますか
	jikokuhyoo wa arimasu ka?
Do you have a room?	部屋はありますか
	heya wa arimasu ka?
Do you have milk?	牛乳はありますか
	gyuunyuu wa arimasu ka?

I/We'd like...	...(動詞) たいです
	...(verb) tai desu
I/We'd like...	...(名詞) が欲しいです
	...(noun) ga hoshii desu
I'd like an ice cream	アイスクリームが欲しいです
	aisukuriimu ga hoshii desu
We'd like to go home	家に帰りたいです
	ie ni kaeritai desu
Another...	...おかわり
	...okawari
Some more...	...もう少し
	...moo sukoshi
Some more bread	パン、もう少し
	pan moo sukoshi
Some more glasses	飲み物、もう少し
	nomimono moo sukoshi
Another Japanese tea	お茶、おかわり
	ocha okawari
Another beer	ビール、おかわり
	biiru okawari
Some more water	お水、もう少し
	omizu moo sukoshi
How much is it?	これはいくらですか
	korewa ikura desu ka?
large	大きい
	ookii
small	小さい
	chiisai

with	と
	to
without	抜きで
	nukide
Where is/are...?	...はどこですか
	... wa doko desu ka
Where is/are the nearest...?	一番近い ... はどこですか
	ichiban chikai ... wa doko desu ka?
How do I get...?	...へはどうやって行きますか
	...ewa dooyatte ikimasu ka?
to the museum	美術館へは
	bijutsukan ewa
to the station	駅へは
	eki ewa
to Kyoto	京都へは
	Kyooto ewa
There is/are...	...があります
	...ga arimasu
There isn't/aren't any...	...がありません
	...ga arimasen
When?	いつ？
	itsu?
At what time...?	何時に...？
	nanjini...?
today	今日
	Kyoo
tomorrow	明日
	ashita

Can I...?	...できますか
	...dekimasu ka?
smoke	喫煙
	kitsuen
taste it	試食
	shishoku
How does this work?	これはどうやって使いますか
	kore wa dooyatte tsukaimasu ka?
What does this mean?	これはどういう意味ですか
	kore wa doo iu imi desu ka?

Work

The Japanese tend to tell you where they work rather than what they do.

What do you do?	お勤めはどちらですか
	otsutome wa dochira desu ka?
How's your work?	仕事はどうですか
	shigoto wa doo desu ka?
I'm...	私は...
	watashi wa...
a doctor	医者です
	isha desu
a manager	経営者です
	keieisha desu

> **Leisure/interests** (p 70) > **Sport** (p 77)

a housewife	主婦です	
	shufu desu	
I work from home	私は在宅勤務です	
	watashi wa zaitaku-kinmu desu	
I'm self-employed	私は自営業です	
	watashi wa jieigyoo desu	

Weather

天気予報	tenki-yohoo	weather forecast
晴れ	hare	fine
悪い	warui	bad
曇り	kumori	cloudy
変わりやすい天気		changeable weather
kawariyasui tenki		

It's sunny	天気がいい
	tenki ga ii
It's muggy	蒸し暑い
	mushiatsui
It's raining	雨が降っている
	ame ga futteiru
It's snowing	雪が降っている
	yuki ga futteiru

It's windy	風が強い	kaze ga tsuyoi
What a lovely day!	なんていい日!	nante iihi!
What awful weather!	なんてひどい天気!	nante hidoi tenki!
What will the weather be like tomorrow?	明日の天気はどうですか	ashitano tenki wa doo desu ka?
Do you think it's going to rain?	雨が降りそうですか	ame ga furisoo desu ka?
It's very hot today	今日はとても暑いです	kyoo wa totemo atsui desu
It's very cold today	今日はとても寒いです	kyoo wa totemo samui desu
Do you think there will be a storm?	嵐になると思いますか	arashi ni naru to omoimasu ka?
Do you think it will snow?	雪になると思いますか	yuki ni naru to omoimasu ka?
Will it be foggy?	霧になると思いますか	kiri ni narv to omoimasu ka?
What is the temperature?	気温は何度ですか	kion wa nando desu ka?

Getting around

Asking the way

反対　hantai	opposite
…の隣　…no tonari	next to...
…の近く　…no chikaku	near to...
信号　shingoo	traffic lights
横断歩道　oodan-hodoo	crossroads
(道路の) 角 (dooro no) kado	corner (of road)

FACE TO FACE

A すみません、駅までどうやって行きますか

sumimasen, eki made dooyatte ikimasu ka?

Excuse me, how do I get to the station?

B まっすぐ行って、一つ目の角を右/
左に曲がってください

massugu itte, hitotsu-me no kado o migi/
hidari ni magatte kudasai

Keep straight on, turn right/left at the first corner

A 遠いですか
tooi desu ka?
Is it far?

B いいえ、200メートル/5分くらいです
iie, nihyaku-meetoru/go-fun kurai desu
No, about 200 metres/five minutes

A ありがとう!
arigatoo!
Thank you!

B どういたしまして
doo itashimashite
You're welcome

We're lost	道に迷いました	
	michi ni mayoimashita	
We're looking for...	...を探しています	
	...o sagashite imasu	
Is this the right way to...?	...に行くのはこれでいいです か	
	...ni iku nowa kore de iidesu ka?	
Can I/we walk there?	そこまで歩けますか	
	soko made arukemasu ka?	

How do I/ we get...?	どうすれば ... に行けますか
	doosureba ... ni ikemasu ka?
to the station	駅に
	eki ni
to the museum	美術館に
	bijutsukan ni
to the shops	お店に
	omise ni
Can you show me on the map?	地図で示してもらえますか
	chizu de shimeshite moraemasu ka?

YOU MAY HEAR...	
下った所 kudatta tokoro	down there
後ろ ushiro	behind
もう一度聞いてください mooichido kiite kudasai	then ask again

Bus and coach

Places such as Kyoto have tourist day passes and bus route maps in English, which you can obtain at a bus station. Local buses usually board from the rear door and if your journey is not covered by a flat fee you may need to pick up a numbered ticket. A board at the front of the bus displays the fares, based on the numbers. You will need to know your destination in Japanese characters. Some buses board from the front door and require you to pay as you enter. Tickets for long/middle distance coach trips, as well as airport limousines, are usually sold at the coach counter or ticketing machine.

FACE TO FACE

A すみません、どのバスが中心部に行きますか

sumimasen, dono basu ga chuushimbu ni ikimasu ka?

Excuse me, which bus goes to the centre?

B 15番です

juugo-ban desu

Number 15

A バス停はどこですか

basutei wa doko desu ka?

Where is the bus stop?

B すぐそこ、右にあります
sugusoko, migi ni arimasu
There, on the right

A どこで乗車券を買えますか
dokode jyooshaken o kaemasu ka?
Where can I buy the tickets?

B 売店で買えます
baiten de kaemasu
At the news-stand

Is there a bus/ tram to...?	...に行くバス/ 路面電車はありますか ...ni iku basu/romen-densha wa arimasu ka?
Where do I/ we catch the bus to...?	どこで ... 行きのバスに乗れますか doko de ... iki no basu ni noremasu ka?
Where do I/ we catch the tram to...?	どこで ... 行きの路面電車に乗れますか doko de ... iki no romen-densha ni noremasu ka?
I/we would like to go to...	...に行きたいんですが ...ni ikitain desu ga
How much is it to go to...?	...までいくらですか ...made ikura desu ka?
the centre	中心部 chuushimbu

the beach	浜辺
	hamabe
How often are the buses to...?	...に行くバスはどのぐらい出ていますか
	...ni iku basu wa donogurai dete imasu ka?
When is the first bus to...?	...行きの始発バスはいつですか
	...iki no shihatsu basu wa itsu desu ka?
When is the last bus to...?	...行きの最終バスはいつですか
	...iki no saishuu basu wa itsu desu ka?
Please tell me when to get off	いつ降りたらいいか教えてください
	itsu oritara iika oshiete kudasai
Please tell me when we are at...	...に着いたら教えてください
	...ni tsuitara oshiete kudasai
Please let me off	すみません、降ろしてください
	sumimasen, oroshite kudasai
I got on at...	...から乗りました
	...kara norimashita
Sorry, I forgot to take a ticket (on entering bus)	すみません、整理券を取りませんでした
	sumimasen, seiriken o torimasen deshita

> **Luggage** (p 94)

ここ/このバス停ですよ koko/kono basu-tei desu yo	This is it/your stop
地下鉄の方が、 　　速いですよ chikatetsu no hooga hayai 　　desu yo	Take the metro, 　　it's quicker

Getting around

Metro

• •

The Japanese metro and train services are clean,
safe and run on time. You can either purchase a
prepaid card or an ordinary ticket from the ticketing
machine. Silver seats are for the elderly or people
with difficulties. Mobile phones need to be on silent
and you must not talk in the carriage. In major cities,
the rush hour (between 7 and 9 am and 5 and 8 pm)
crush can be really bad. Some trains have women-
only carriages. The Japanese metro system is very
similar to the one in London. The first thing you
must do is obtain a metro map which indicates all
the lines and stops.

入口	iriguchi	entrance
出口	deguchi	way out/exit

Can I get a seat reservation please?	座席の予約をお願いします zaseki no yoyaku o onegai shimasu
Where can I get a ticket?	切符はどこで買えますか kippu wa doko de kaemasu ka?
Where is the nearest metro station?	一番近い地下鉄の駅はどこで すか ichiban chikai chikatetsu no eki wa doko desu ka?
How does the ticket machine work?	券売機はどうやって使います か kenbaiki wa dooyatte tsukaimasu ka?
I'm going to...	...に行きます ...ni ikimasu
Do you have a map of the metro?	地下鉄の地図はありますか chikatetsu no chizu wa arimasu ka?
How do I get to...?	どうやって ... に行きますか dooyatte ... ni ikimasu ka?
Do I have to change?	乗り換えはありますか norikae wa arimasu ka?
Does this go to...?	これは ... に行きますか kore wa ... ni ikimasu ka?
Which line is it for...?	...行きは何線ですか ...iki wa nani-sen desu ka

> **Luggage** (p 94)

Which platform is it for...?	...行きは何番線ですか
What is the next stop?	...iki wa nan-bansen desu ka
	次の駅はどこですか
	tsugi no eki wa doko desu ka?
Excuse me!	すみません!
	sumimasen!
Please let me out	降ろしてください
	oroshite kudasai

Train

You will find **Midori no madoguchi** in major train stations where you can exchange Japan Rail Passes to make seat bookings etc. A JR pass can get you a considerable way around Japan. Details can be found at **www.japanrailpass.net**.

各駅停車　kakueki teisha	**slow stopping train** (stops at all stations)
快速/特別快速電車 kaisoku/tokubetsu kaisoku densha	**local train** (stops at selected stations)
準急/急行電車 junkyuu/kyuukoo densha	**intercity** (stops at main intercity stations: supplement)

特急電車　tokkyuu densha	intercity (stops at main intercity stations: supplement)
新幹線　こだま/ひかり shinkansen kodama/hikari	high-speed intercity **bullet train** (JR pass accepted)
新幹線　のぞみ shinkansen nozomi	high-speed intercity **bullet train** (JR pass not accepted)
プラットフォーム puratto foomu	platform
窓口　madoguchi	ticket office
時刻表　jikokuhyoo	timetable
遅れ　okure	delay (appears on train noticeboards)
手荷物一時預かり tenimotsu ichiji azukari	left luggage

FACE TO FACE

次の … 行きの電車は何時ですか
tsugi no … iki no densha wa nan-ji desu ka?
What time is the next train to...?

17時10分です
juushichi-ji juppun desu
At 17.10

A 切符を3枚ください

kippu o san-mai kudasai

I'd like 3 tickets, please

B 片道ですか、往復ですか

katamichi desu ka, oofuku desu ka?

Single or return?

Where is the station?	駅はどこですか
	eki wa doko desu ka?
to...	...行き
	...iki
a single	片道一枚
	katamichi ichi-mai
two returns	往復二枚
	oofuku ni-mai
reserved seat	指定席
	shitei-seki
non-reserved seat	自由席
	jiyuu-seki
first class	グリーン車
	guriin-sha
standard class	普通車
	futsuu-sha
smoking	喫煙
	kitsuen
non smoking	禁煙
	kinen

I want to book a seat on the bullet train to Tokyo	東京まで新幹線の指定席を予約したいんですが
	Tookyoo made shinkansen no shitei-seki o yoyaku shitain desu ga
Do I have to change?	乗り換えがありますか
	norikae ga arimasu ka?
How long is there to wait for the connection?	乗り換え時間はどのくらいありますか
	norikae-jikan wa donokurai arimasu ka?
Is this the train for...?	これは … 行きの電車ですか
	kore wa … iki no densha desu ka?
Why is the train delayed?	なぜ電車は遅れているのですか
	naze densha wa okurete iruno desu ka?
When will it leave?	いつ出発しますか
	itsu shuppatsu shimasu ka?
Does it stop at...?	…に停まりますか
	…ni tomarimasu ka?
When does it arrive in...?	…にはいつ着きますか
	…niwa itsu tsukimasu ka?
Please tell me when we get to...	…に着いたら教えてください
	…ni tsuitara oshiete kudasai

> **Luggage** (p 94)

Is there a restaurant car?	食堂車はありますか
	shokudoo-sha wa arimasu ka?
Is this seat free?	この席は空いていますか
	konoseki wa aite imasu ka?
Excuse me! (to get past)	すみません!
	sumimasen!

Taxi

Japanese taxis are safe, clean and operate on meters. The basic fee is based on the vehicle size. It can be rather expensive but there is no need to tip. There are taxi stands at stations and major hotels but taxis can also be hailed from the roadside. You can identify whether a taxi is available by the sign 空車 (kuusha) displayed in the front windscreen. All the doors are automatically operated by the driver. A receipt can be requested if necessary.

I want a taxi	タクシーに乗りたいです
	takushii ni noritai desu
Where can I get a taxi?	タクシー乗り場はどこですか
	takushii noriba wa doko desu ka?
Please order me a taxi	タクシーを呼んでください
	takushii o yonde kudasai

now	今
	ima
for...(time)	...(時) に
	...(ji) ni
How much will it cost to go to...?	...までいくらかかりますか
	...made ikura kakarimasu ka?
How long will it take?	どのくらいかかりますか
	donokurai kakarimasu ka?
vacant (car)	空車
	kuusha
to the station please	駅までお願いします
	eki made onegai shimasu
to the airport please	空港までお願いします
	kuukoo made onegai shimasu
to this address please	この住所までお願いします
	kono juusho made onegai shimasu
How much is it?	いくらですか
	ikura desu ka?
Can I have a receipt please?	レシートをお願いします
	reshiito o onegai shimasu
Keep the change	おつりは結構です
	otsuri wa kekkoo desu
Sorry, I don't have any change	すみません、小銭がありません
	sumimasen, kozeni ga arimasen
I'm in a hurry	急いでいます
	isoide imasu

Taxi

I have to catch...	...に乗らなくてはいけないん です
	...ni noranakutewa ikenain desu
a train	電車
	densha
a plane	飛行機
	hikooki

Boat and ferry

Japan Railways (JR) run ferry services on certain routes where the JR Pass can be used. There is a good ferry network in Japan linking the various islands. Ferries can be used as an alternative to trains if you wish to travel between the islands and have time to spare. During the holidays some lines can be very busy, so if you are driving it is advisable to book a place in advance.

Do you have a timetable?	時刻表はありますか jikokuhyoo wa arimasu ka?
Is there a car ferry to...?	...に行くカーフェリーはあり ますか
	...ni iku kaa-ferii wa arimasu ka?
How much is a ticket...?	切符はいくらですか kippu wa ikura desu ka?

single	片道
	katamichi
return	往復
	oofuku
How much is it for a car and ... people?	車と人が … 人でいくらですか
	kuruma to hito ga ... nin de ikura desu ka?
one person	一人
	hitori
two people	二人
	futari
three people	三人
	san-nin
Where does the boat leave from?	ボートはどこから出ますか
	booto wa doko kara demasu ka?
Are there any boat trips?	遊覧船はありますか
	yuuransen wa arimasu ka?
of the Tokyo bay	東京湾の
	Tookyoo-wan no
When is the next boat?	次の船は何時ですか
	tsugi no fune wa nan-ji desu ka?
How long does the trip take?	遊覧はどのくらいかかりますか
	yuuran wa donokurai kakarimasu ka?

これが最終便です kore ga saishuu-bin desu	This is the last boat
今日はやっていません kyoo wa yatte imasen	There is no service today
車は何ですか kuruma wa nan desu ka?	What type of car do you have?

Air travel

• •

At the airport, most signs are written in both Japanese and English. All the airport staff understand and speak some English. You can find airport details by visiting **www.narita-airport.or.jp** or **www.kansai-airport.or.jp**.

到着	toochaku	arrivals
出発	shuppatsu	departures
国際	kokusai	international
国内	kokunai	domestic
搭乗口	toojooguchi	boarding gate

How do I/we go to...?	...にはどうやって行けばいいですか
	...niwa dooyatte ikeba ii desu ka?
to the airport	空港には
	kuukoo niwa
to town	街には
	machi niwa
to the hotel...	...ホテルには
	...hoteru niwa
to the ... airport	...空港には
	...kuukoo niwa
Is there a bus to the airport?	空港行きのバスはありますか
	kuukoo iki no basu wa arimasu ka?
How much is it by taxi to...?	...までタクシーでいくらですか
	...made takushii de ikura desu ka?
Where is the check-in desk for...?	...のチックインカウンターはどこですか
	...no chekku in kauntaa wa doko desu ka?
Which turn table is the luggage for the flight from...?	...から着いた荷物はどのターンテーブルですか
	...kara tsuita nimotsu wa dono taanteeburu desu ka?
Where can I change some money?	お金の両替はどこでできますか
	okane no ryoogae wa doko de dekimasu ka?

Air travel

> **Luggage** (p 94)

| ...番ゲートから搭乗します ...ban geeto kara toojoo shimasu | Boarding will take place at gate number... |
| 番ゲートまで至急お進み ください ...ban geeto made sikyuu osusumi kudasai | Go immediately to gate number... |

Customs control

UK, US, Canadian and Australian visitors to Japan do not require a visa for short business trips and holidays. During your stay, you are not allowed to work. It is advisable that you carry proof of identity at all times, so make sure that you always carry your passport.

Visit **www.narita-airport-customs.go.jp** to find out about duty free allowance.

日本人帰国 nihon-jin kikoku	Japanese returning to the country
外国人入国 gaikoku-jin nyuukoku	Non-Japanese entering the country
税関　zeikan	customs

Do I have to pay duty on this?	これに税金がかかりますか
	kore ni zeikin ga kakarimasu ka?
It's for my own personal use	私が使う物です
	watashi ga tsukau mono desu
It's a present	プレゼントです
	purezento desu
I have nothing to declare	申告する物はありません
	shinkoku suru mono wa arimasen
We are on our way to... (if in transit through a country)	...に行く途中経由です
	...ni iku tochuu keiyu desu
The child/children	こども/こどもたち
	kodomo/kodomotachi
is/are also on this passport	もこのパスポートです
	mo kono pasupooto desu
My passport	私のパスポート
	watashi no pasupooto
My visa	私のビザ
	watashi no biza
I came here on...	...で来ました
	...de kimashita
holiday	休暇
	kyuuka
business	仕事
	shigoto

Driving

Car hire

| 運転免許証
unten-menkyoshoo | driving licence |
| 総合保険　soogoohoken | fully comprehensive insurance |

Driving

I want to hire a car	車をかりたいです kuruma o karitai desu
for ... days	...日 ...nichi
with automatic gears	オートマ車 ootoma sha
What are your rates...?	...料金はいくらですか ...ryookin wa ikura desu ka?
per day	一日の ichinichi no
per week	一週間の isshuukan no

How much is the deposit?	保証金はいくらですか hoshookin wa ikura desu ka?
Do you take credit cards?	クレジットカードは使えますか kurejitto kaado wa tsukaemasu ka?
Is there a charge per mile/ kilometre?	走行距離の支払いはありますか sookoo-kyori no siharai wa arimasu ka?
How much is it?	いくらですか ikura desu ka?
Does the price include fully comprehensive insurance?	この金額は総合保険料を含んでいますか kono kingaku wa soogoohoken-ryoo o fukunde imasu ka?
Must I return the car here?	車はここに返さなければいけませんか kuruma wa kokoni kaesanakereba ikemasen ka?
By what time?	何時までにですか nanji made ni desu ka?
I'd like to leave it in...	私は … に置いてきたいです watashi wa ... ni oite kitai desu

| 車はガソリンを満タンにして返してください
kuruma wa gasorin o mantan ni shite kaeshite kudasai | Please return the car with a full tank |

Driving

Can I/we park here?	ここに駐車してもいいですか kokoni chuusha sitemo ii desu ka?
How long for?	どのくらいまで? donokurai made?
Which junction is it for...?	...に行くにはどのジャンクションですか ...ni iku niwa dono jankushon desu ka?
Do I/we need snow chains?	チェーンは必要ですか cheen wa hitsuyoo desu ka?

Petrol

• •

In Japan, the majority of petrol stations are manned by attendants who not only fill up the tank for you but also wipe the windows and check the water.

ハイオク	haioku	4 star
ディーゼル	diizeru	diesel
無鉛	muen	unleaded
有鉛	yuuen	leaded

Fill it up, please	満タンにしてください
	mantan ni site kudasai
Please check...	...をチェックしてください
	...o chekku shite kudasai
the oil	オイル
	oiru
the water	水
	mizu
3000 yen worth of unleaded petrol	3000円分の無鉛ガソリン
	sanzen en bun no muen gasorin
Where is...?	...はどこですか
	...wa doko desu ka?
the air line	エアー
	eaa
water	水
	mizu

| Can I pay by credit card? | クレジットカードで払えますか
kurejitto kaado de haraemasu ka? |

YOU MAY HEAR...

| オイル/水が必要です
oiru/mizu ga hitsuyoo desu | You need some oil/
some water |
| 全て大丈夫です
subete daijoobu desu | Everything is OK |

Breakdown

If you break down, the emergency telephone number for the Japanese equivalent of the AA (JAF – Japan Automobile Federation) is **0570-00-8139** or # (pound key) **8139**

Can you help me?	助けてもらえますか tasukete moraemasu ka?
My car has broken down	車が故障してしまいました kuruma ga koshooshite shimaimashita
I've run out of petrol	ガソリンがきれてしまいました gasorin ga kirete shimaimashita

Can you tow me to the nearest garage?	最寄のガソリンスタンドまで引っぱって行ってもらえますか
	moyori no gasorin-sutando made hippatte itte moraemasu ka?
Do you have parts for a (make of car)...?	...の部品がありますか
	...no buhin ga arimasu ka?
There's something wrong with the...	...に何かおかしいところがあります
	...ni nanika okashii tokoro ga arimasu
Can you replace...?	...を交換できますか
	...o kookan dekimasu ka?

Car parts

The ... isn't/aren't working properly	...の調子が悪いです
	...no chooshi ga warui desu

accelerator	アクセル	akuseru
alternator	オルタネーター	orutaneetaa
battery	バッテリー	batterii
bonnet	ボンネット	bonnetto
brakes	ブレーキ	bureeki
choke	チョーク	chooku

clutch	クラッチ	kurattchi
distributor	配電器	haidenki
engine	エンジン	enjin
exhaust	エキゾースト	ekizoosuto
fuse	ヒューズ	hyuuzu
gears	ギア	gia
handbrake	ハンドブレーキ	hando bureeki
headlights	ヘッドライト	heddo raito
ignition	点火装置	tenka soochi
indicator	方向指示器	hookoo shijiki
points	ポイント	pointo
radiator	ラジエーター	rajieetaa
reverse gear	バックギア	bakku gia
seat belt	シートベルト	shiito beruto
spark plug	点火プラグ	tenka puragu
steering	ステアリング	sutearingu
steering wheel	ステアリング　ホイール	sutearingu hoiiru
tyre	タイヤ	taiya
wheel	車輪	sharin
windscreen	フロントガラス	furonto garasu
windscreen washer	ウインドウウォッシャー	uindoo wosshaa
windscreen wiper	ワイパー	waipaa

48

Road signs

no thoroughfare

closed to pedestrians

stopping permitted

centre line

drive slowly

stop

bicycle crossing

minimum speed

pedestrian
crossing

two-step right turn
for motorcycles

stop line

safety zone

Staying somewhere

Hotel (booking)

Japan offers a wide choice of places to stay, from western-style hotels to traditional Japanese inns. Capsule hotels offer minimum sleeping space on multiple levels, but have all the facilities and are good value for money.

シングルルーム shinguru ruumu	single room
ダブルルーム daburu ruumu	double room
洋室　yooshitsu	western-style room
和室　washitsu	Japanese-style room
大人の人数 otona no ninzuu	number of adults
子供の人数 kodomo no ninzuu	number of children

A シングル/ダブルルームを予約したいんですが
shinguru/daburu ruumu o yoyaku shitain desu ga
I'd like to book a single/double room

B 何泊ですか
nampaku desu ka?
For how many nights?

A 一泊です/...泊です/...から...までです
ippaku desu/...haku (paku) desu/...kara...made desu
For one night/...nights/from...till...

How much is it per night/ per week?	一泊/一週間いくらですか ippaku/isshuukan ikura desu ka?
Do you have a room for tonight?	今夜泊まれますか konya tomaremasu ka?
with bath	お風呂付き ofuro tsuki
with shower	シャワー付き shawaa tsuki
with a double bed	ダブルベッド付き daburu beddo tsuki
with twin beds and an extra bed for a child	ツインベッドと子供のための エクストラベッド tsuin beddo to kodomo no tameno ekusutra beddo

Is breakfast included?	朝ごはんは含まれていますか
	asa gohan wa fukumarete imasu ka?
Have you got anything cheaper?	もう少し安いのはないですか
	moosukoshi yasui no wa naidesu ka?
I'd like to see the room	部屋を見せてもらえますか
	heya o misete moraemasu ka

YOU MAY HEAR...

満室です	We're full
manshitsu desu	
お名前をお願いします	Your name, please
onamae o onegai shimasu	
...の確認をお願いします	Please confirm...
...no kakunin o onegai shimasu	
メールで	by e-mail
meeru de	
ファックスで	by fax
fakkusu de	

Hotel desk

The Japan National Tourist Organization and Tourist Information Centre can help with finding accommodation. Visit **www.jnto.go.jp**.

I booked a room...	...の部屋を予約しました
	...no heya o yoyaku shimashita
in the name of...	...の名前で
	...no namae de
Where can I park the car?	どこに車を停められますか
	doko ni kuruma o tomeraremasu ka?
What time is...?	...は何時ですか
	...wa nanji desu ka?
dinner	夕食
	yuushoku
breakfast	朝食
	chooshoku
The key, please	鍵をお願いします
	kagi o onegai shimasu
Room number...	部屋番号は...
	heya bangoo wa...
Are there any messages for me?	私あてのメッセージはありますか
	watashi ate no messeeji wa arimasu ka?

Staying somewhere

54

Can I send a fax?	ファックスを送れますか
	fakkusu o okuremasu ka?
I'm leaving tomorrow	明日発ちます
	ashita tachimasu
Please prepare the bill	清算をお願いします
	seisan o onegai shimasu

Camping

ごみ gomi	rubbish
飲料水 inryoosui	drinking water
コンセント konsento	electric point

Is there ... on the campsite?	キャンプ場に ... はありますか
	kyanpujoo ni ... wa arimasu ka?
a restaurant	レストラン
	resutoran
a self-service café	セルフサービスの食堂
	serufu-saabisu no shokudoo
Do you have any vacancies?	空きはありますか
	aki wa arimasu ka?
How much is it...?	...いくらですか
	...ikura desu ka?
per night	一泊
	ippaku

per tent	テントあたり
	tento atari
per caravan	キャラバンあたり
	kyaraban atari
per person	一人あたり
	hitori atari
Does the price include...?	...の料金は含まれていますか
	...no ryookin wa fukumarete imasu ka?
showers	シャワー
	shawaa
hot water	お湯
	oyu
electricity	電気
	denki
We'd like to stay for ... nights	私たちは ... 泊したいです
	watashitachi wa ... haku (paku) shitai desu

Self-catering

....

Who do we contact if there are problems?	何か問題があった場合、誰に連絡すればいいですか
	nani ka mondai ga atta baai, dare ni renraku sureba ii desu ka?
How does the heating work?	ヒーターはどうやって使いますか
	hiitaa wa dooyatte tsukaimasu ka?
Is there always hot water?	お湯はいつでもでますか
	oyu wa itudemo demasu ka?
Where is the nearest supermarket?	最寄のスーパーはどこですか
	moyori no suupaa wa doko desu ka?
Where do we leave the rubbish?	ごみはどこに捨てればいいですか
	gomi wa dokoni sutereba ii desu ka?

> **Sightseeing and tourist office** (p 70)

Shopping

Shopping phrases

Opening hours are approximately 10.00 am to
6.30 pm with slightly longer opening hours at the
weekends, in summer and at the end of the year.
Some supermarkets are open 24 hours a day.

FACE TO FACE

A 何をお求めですか

nani o omotome desu ka?

What would you like?

B …はありますか

…wa arimasu ka?

Do you have...?

A はい、こちらになります。他に何か

hai, kochira ni narimasu. hoka ni nani ka?

Certainly, here you are. Anything else?

Where is...?	...はどこですか
	...wa doko desu ka?
I'm just looking	見ているだけです
	miteiru dake desu
I'm looking for a present for...	...へのプレゼントを探しています
	...eno purezento o sagashite imasu
my mother	私の母
	watashi no haha
a child	子ども
	kodomo
Where can I buy...?	...はどこで買えますか
	...wa doko de kaemasu ka?
shoes	靴
	kutsu
gifts	ギフト
	gifuto
Do you have anything...?	もう少し ... ものはありますか
	moo sukoshi ... mono wa arimasu ka?
larger	大きい
	ookii
smaller	小さい
	chiisai

Shops

セール　seeru	sale	
割引　waribiki	discount	
祝日休業 shukujitsu kyuugyoo	closed for holidays	

baker's	パン屋	pan-ya
bookshop	本屋	honya
butcher's	肉屋	niku-ya
cake shop	ケーキ屋	keeki-ya
clothes	洋服屋	yoofuku-ya
department store	デパート	depaato
fruit shop	果物屋	kudamono-ya
gifts	贈り物	okurimono
grocer's	食料雑貨商	shokuryoo zakka shoo
hairdresser's	美容院	biyooin
newsagent	新聞販売所	shimbun hambai-jo
optician	メガネ屋	megane-ya
cosmetic shop	化粧品屋	keshoohin-ya
pharmacy	薬局	yakkyoku
photographic shop	写真屋	shashin-ya

shoe shop	靴屋	kutsu-ya
sports shop	スポーツ ショップ	supootsu shoppu
supermarket	スーパー	suupaa
tobacconist's	タバコ屋	tabako-ya
toys	おもちゃ屋	omocha-ya

Food (general)

biscuits	ビスケット	bisuketto
bread	パン	pan
bread (for toast)	食パン	shoku pan
sweet bread	菓子パン	kashi pan
butter	バター	bataa
cheese	チーズ	chiizu
chicken	チキン	chikin
coffee	コーヒー	koohii
cream	クリーム	kuriimu
crisps	ポテトチップス	poteto-chippusu
eggs	たまご	tamago
fish	魚	sakana
ham	ハム	hamu
ham (uncured)	生ハム	nama-hamu
herbal tea	ハーブティー	haabu tii
jam	ジャム	jamu

margarine	マーガリン	maagarin
marmalade	マーマレード	maamareedo
milk	ミルク	miruku
oil	油	abura
orange juice	オレンジジュース	orenji juusu
pepper	こしょう	koshoo
salt	しお	shio
sugar	さとう	satoo
Japanese tea	お茶	ocha
English tea	紅茶	koocha
vinegar	酢	su
yoghurt	ヨーグルト	yooguruto

Food (fruit and veg)

Fruit

apples	りんご	ringo
apricots	アプリコット	apurikotto
bananas	バナナ	banana
cherries	さくらんぼ	sakuranbo
grapefruit	グレープフルーツ	gureepu furuutsu
grapes	ぶどう	budoo

 > **Measurements and quantities** (p 112)

lemon	レモン	remon
melon	メロン	meron
oranges	オレンジ	orenji
peaches	桃	momo
pears	梨	nashi
plums	すもも	sumomo
raspberries	ラズベリー	razuberii
strawberries	いちご	ichigo
watermelon	すいか	suika

Vegetables

asparagus	アスパラガス	asuparagasu
aubergine	なす	nasu
carrots	にんじん	ninjin
cauliflower	カリフラワー	karifurawaa
celery	セロリ	serori
courgettes	ズッキーニ	zukkiini
cucumber	きゅうり	kyuuri
garlic	にんにく	ninniku
leeks	ねぎ	negi
mushrooms	きのこ	kinoko
onions	たまねぎ	tamanegi
peas	エンドウ	endoo
pepper	ピーマン	piiman
potatoes	じゃがいも	jagaimo
runner beans	インゲン	ingen

salad	サラダ	sarada
spinach	ほうれん草	hoorensoo
tomatoes	トマト	tomato

Clothes

. . . .

women's sizes		men's sizes		shoe sizes			
UK	Japan	UK	Japan	UK	Japan	UK	Japan
8	7	34	S	2	22	7	25.5
10	9	36	M	3	22.5	8	26.5
12	11	38	L	4	23	9	27.5
14	13	40	LL/XL	5	24	10	28
16	15			6	24.5	11	28.5
18	17						

FACE TO FACE

A 試着してみてもいいですか

shichaku shite mitemo ii desu ka?

May I try this on?

B どうぞ、こちらに

doozo, kochira ni

Please come this way

S/M/Lサイズはありますか
esu/emu/eru saizu wa arimasu ka?
Do you have a small/medium/large size?

サイズは何ですか
saizu wan an desu ka
What size (clothes) do you take?

bigger	もっと大きい
	motto ookii
smaller	もっと小さい
	motto chiisai
in other colours	他の色で
	hoka no iro de

YOU MAY HEAR...

靴のサイズはいくつです か	What shoe size do you take?
kutsu no saizu wa ikutsu desu ka?	
この色はこのサイズしか ありません	In this colour we only have this size
kono iro wa kono saizu shika arimasen	

Clothes

> **Paying** (p 92) > **Numbers** (p 115)

Clothes (articles)

blouse	ブラウス	burausu
coat	コート	kooto
dress	ドレス	doresu
jacket	ジャケット	jaketto
jumper	ジャンパー	jampaa
knickers	パンティー	pantii
shirt	シャツ	shatsu
shorts	半ズボン	hanzubon
skirt	スカート	sukaato
socks	ソックス	sokkusu
swimsuit	水着	mizugi
t-shirt	Tシャツ	tii shatsu
trousers	ズボン	zubon

Shopping

Maps and guides

....

キオスク	kiosuku	kiosk
週刊誌	shuukanshi	a weekly magazine
新聞	shimbun	newspaper

Do you have a map...?	...の地図はありますか
	...no chizu wa arimasu ka?
of the town	町の
	machi no
of the region	この地域の
	kono chiiki no
Can you show me where ... is on the map?	この地図で ... はどこにありますか
	kono chizu de ... wa doko ni arimasu ka?
Do you have a ... in English?	英語の ... はありますか
	eigo no ... wa arimasu ka
a guidebook	ガイドブック
	gaidobukku
a leaflet	パンフレット
	panfuretto
Do you have any English...?	英語の ... はありますか
	eigo no ... wa arimasu ka

> **Asking the way** (p 22)
> **Sightseeing and tourist office** (p 70)

newspapers	新聞
	shimbun
books	本
	hon

Post office

....

| 郵便局　yuubinkyoku | **post office** |
| 切手　kitte | **stamps** |

Post office opening hours can vary but they are usually open from 9.00 am to 5.00 pm, Monday to Friday. Some post offices in the main cities stay open until around 7.00 pm and at weekends.

Where is the post office?	郵便局はどこですか
	yuubinkyoku wa doko desu ka?
When does it open?	いつ開きますか
	itsu akimasu ka?
Which is the counter...?	...カウンターはどこですか
	...kauntaa wa doko desu ka?
for stamps	切手の
	kitte no
for parcels	小包の
	kozutsumi no

> **Money** (p 90) > **Paying** (p 92)

6 stamps for postcards...	...葉書用の切手6枚
	...hagaki-yoo no kitte roku-mai
first class post	速達
	sokutatsu
for Britain	イギリスに
	igirisu ni
for America	アメリカに
	amerika ni
for Australia	オーストラリアに
	oosutoraria ni

YOU MAY HEAR...

| タバコ屋で切手を買うこ とができます tabako-ya de kitte o kau koto ga dekimasu | You can buy stamps at the tobacconist |

Photos

• •

A tape for this camcorder	このビデオカメラのテープ
	kono bideokamera no teepu
Do you have batteries for this camera?	このカメラのバッテリーはあ りますか
	kono kamera no batterii wa arimasu ka?

Leisure

Sightseeing and tourist office

....

The Japan National Tourist Organisation has a great deal of information. Visit **www.jnto.go.jp**.

Where is the tourist office?	観光案内所はどこですか kankoo-annai-jo wa doko desu ka?
What can we visit in the area?	このエリアでは何を見ることができますか kono eria dewa nani o miru koto ga dekimasu ka?
in two hours	二時間で ni-jikan de
Have you any leaflets?	何かパンフレットはありますか nani ka panfuretto wa arimasu ka?
Are there any excursions?	何か周遊ツアーはありますか nani ka shuuyuu tsuaa wa arimasu ka?
We'd like to go to...	私たちは … に行きたいです watashitachi wa ... ni ikitai desu

70

How much does it cost to get in?	入るのにいくらかかりますか
	hairu noni ikura kakarimasu ka?
Are there reductions for...?	...の割引はありますか
	...no waribiki wa arimasu ka?
children	子供
	kodomo
students	学生
	gakusei
over 60s	60歳以上
	rokujussai-ijoo

Entertainment

What is there to do in the evenings?	そこでは夜は何ができますか
	soko dewa yoru wa nani ga dekimasu ka?
Do you have a programme of events?	イベントのプログラムはありますか
	ibento no puroguramu wa arimasu ka?
Is there anything for children?	子供のためのものはありますか
	kodomo no tame no mono wa arimasu ka?

> **Maps and guides** (p 67)

Leisure/interests

Where can I/ we go...? ...はどこでできますか
...wa doko de dekimasu ka?

fishing 釣り
tsuri

walking 散歩
sampo

Are there any good beaches near here? この近くにいい浜辺はありますか
kono chikaku ni ii hamabe wa arimasu ka?

Is there a swimming pool? スイミングプールはありますか
suimingu puuru wa arimasu ka?

Music

Are there any good concerts on? 何かいいコンサートはありますか
nani ka ii konsaato wa arimasu ka?

Where can I/we get tickets for the concert? コンサートのチケットはどこで買えますか
konsaato no chiketto wa doko de kaemasu ka

Where can I/we hear some classical music?	どこでクラシックを聴けますか doko de kurashikku o kikemasu ka?
Where can I/we hear some jazz?	どこでジャズを聴けますか doko de jazu o kikemasu ka?

Cinema

. . . .

What's on at the cinema (name of cinema)?	…映画館では何を上映していますか …eigakan dewa nani o jooei shite imasu ka?
What time does the film start?	映画は何時に始まりますか eiga wa nan-ji ni hajimarimasu ka?
How much are the tickets?	チケットはいくらですか chiketto wa ikura desu ka?
Two for the (give time of performance) showing	…のショーに二人分 …ji no shoo ni futari-bun

Theatre/opera

Major hotels can get theatre and opera tickets for you, or you can buy them at ticketing offices such as **Pureigaido** and **Midori no madoguchi** in stations and travel agencies. You can also search and buy any tickets on the internet. If you are lucky enough to be able to obtain a **Kabuki** (Japanese Opera) ticket, it is definitely worth going. English translation is available.

General theaters/concert halls

S席	esu-seki	Superior seat
A席	ee-seki	Class A seat
B席	bii-seki	Standard seat

Kabuki theatres

一等	ittoo	First class seat
二等	nitoo	Second class seat
三階A	sangai ee	Second floor seat
桟敷	sajiki	circle
席	seki	seat
クローク	kurooku	cloakroom

What is on at the theatre?	劇場では何をやっていますか
	gekijoo dewa nani o yatte imasu ka?
What prices are the tickets?	チケットの値段はいくらですか
	chiketto no nedan wa ikura desu ka?
I'd like two tickets...	...のチケットを2枚ください
	...no chiketto o ni-mai kudasai
for tonight	今夜の
	konya no
for tomorrow night	明日の夜の
	ashita no yoru no
for the 3rd of August	8月3日の
	hachi gatsu mikka no
When does the performance begin?	上演はいつ始まりますか
	jooen wa itsu hajimari masu ka?
When does the performance end?	上演はいつ終わりますか
	jooen wa itsu owari masu ka?

YOU MAY HEAR...

もう開演していますので 入場できません	You can't go in as the performance has started
moo kaien shite imasu node nyuujoo dekimasen	
休憩のときに入場できます	You may enter at the interval
kyuukei no toki ni nyuujoo dekimasu	

Television

Leisure

リモコン　rimokon	remote control
スイッチを入れます suitchi o iremasu	to switch on
スイッチを切ります suitchi o kirimasu	to switch off
シリーズ　shiriizu	series
連続ドラマ renzoku-dorama	soap
ニュース　nyuusu	news
マンガ　manga	cartoons

Where is the television?	テレビはどこにありますか terebi wa doko ni arimasu ka?
How do you switch it on?	スイッチはどうやって入れますか suitchi wa dooyatte iremasu ka?
What is on television?	テレビでは何をやっていますか terebi dewa nani o yatte imasu ka?
When is the news?	ニュースはいつですか nyuusu wa itsu desu ka?

Do you have any English-language channels?	何か英語の番組はありますか
	nani ka eigo no bangumi wa arimasu ka?
Do you have any English videos?	何か英語のビデオはありますか
	nani ka eigo no bideo wa arimasu ka?

Sport

Where can we...?	...はどこでできますか
	...wa doko de dekimasu ka?
go swimming	水泳
	suiei
go jogging	ジョギング
	jogingu
Do I have to be a member?	会員にならなくてはいけませんか
	kaiin ni naranakutewa ikemasen ka?
How much is it per hour?	1時間いくらですか
	ichi-jikan ikura desu ka
Can we hire...?	...を借りられますか
	...o kariraremasu ka?

rackets	ラケット
golf clubs	raketto
	ゴルフクラブ
	gorufukurabu
We'd like to see (name team) play	私たちは … のプレーを見たいです
	watashitachi wa … no puree o mitai desu
Where can I/we get tickets for the game?	どこで試合のチケットを買えますか
	doko de shiai no chiketto o kaemasu ka?

| 試合のチケットは売り切れました | There are no tickets left for the game |
| shiai no chiketto wa urikiremashita | |

Skiing

. . . .

クロスカントリースキー kurosukantorii sukii	cross-country skiing
リフト券 rifuto ken	ski pass

I want to hire skis	スキー板を借りたいです
	sukii ita o karitai desu
Does the price include...?	...の値段は含まれていますか
	...no nedan wa fukumarete
	imasu ka?
boots	ブーツ
	buutsu
poles	ストック
	sutokku
How much is a pass...?	...券の値段はいくらですか
	...ken no nedan wa ikura desu ka?
daily	一日券
	ichinichi ken
weekly	一週間券
	isshuukan ken
What time is the last ascent lift?	最後の上りのリフトは何時で すか
	saigo no nobori no rifuto wa nan-ji
	desu ka?

> **Emergencies** (p 100) > **Sport** (p 77)

Skiing

| Can you adjust my bindings? | 締め具を調節してもらえますか |
| | simegu o choosetsu site moraemasu ka? |

YOU MAY HEAR...

今までにスキーをしたことはありますか ima made ni sukii o shita koto wa arimasu ka?	Have you ever skied before?
板の長さはどのくらいがいいですか itano nagasa wa donokurai ga ii desu ka?	What length skis do you want?
ブーツのサイズはいくつですか buutsu no saizu wa ikutsu desu ka?	What is your boot size?
スキーレッスンを受けたいですか sukii ressun o uketai desu ka?	Do you want skiing lessons?

Walking

. . . .

Are there any guided walks?	ガイドウォークはありますか
	gaido wooku wa arimasu ka?
Do you know any good walks?	何かいいウォーキングコースはありますか
	nanika ii wookingu koosu wa arimasu ka?
How many kilometres is the walk?	ウォーキングコースは何キロですか
	wookingu koosu wa nan kiro desu ka?
Is it very steep?	それは急ですか
	sore wa kyuu desu ka?
How long will it take?	どのくらいかかりますか
	donokurai kakarimasu ka?
Is there a map of the walk?	ウォーキングコースの地図はありますか
	wookingu koosu no chizu wa arimasu ka?
We'd like to go climbing	山登りに行きたいです
	yamanobori ni ikitai desu
Do you have a detailed map of the area?	この付近の詳しい地図がありますか
	kono fukin no kuwashii chizu ga arimasu ka?

> **Maps and guides** (p 67)

Communications

Telephone and mobile

● ●

The international dialling code for Japan is **00 81**
plus the Japanese town or area code less the first **0**,
for example, Tokyo **(0)33**, Osaka **(0)6**. Japanese
public telephones are very good and you can make
an international call from a grey or green public
telephone. You will need to use 100 yen coins or buy
an appropriate telephone card from a vending
machine. Be careful to purchase the correct card as
there are various types available and the most
common cards are for local and national calls only.

テレホンカード terehon-kaado	phonecard
公衆電話　　kooshuu denwa	public phone
携帯 (電話)　keitai (denwa)	mobile

I want to make a phone call	電話をかけたいです
	den wa o kaketai desu
Where can I buy a phonecard?	どこでテレホンカードを買えますか
	doko de terehon-kaado o kaemasu ka?
A phonecard	テレホンカード
	terehon-kaado
for ... yen	…円分
	…en bun
Do you have a mobile?	携帯 (電話) を持っていますか
	keitai (denwa) o motte imasu ka?
What is the number of your mobile?	あなたの携帯 (電話) は何番ですか
	anata no keitai (denwa) wa namban desu ka?
My mobile number is...	私の携帯 (電話) は … 番です
	watashi no keitai (denwa) wa … ban desu
Mr Brun, please	ブルンさん お願いします
	burun-san onegai shimasu
extension...	内線…
	naisen…

A こんにちは
konnichiwa
Hello

B ...さん、お願いします
...san, onegai shimasu
I'd like to speak to..., please

A どちらさまですか
dochirasama desu ka?
Who's calling?

B アンジェラです
anjera desu
It's Angela

A 少々お待ちください...
shooshoo omachi kudasai...
Just a moment...

Can I speak to...?	...さん、おねがいします
	...san, onegai shimasu
I'll call back later	後でかけ直します
	ato de kakenaoshimasu
I'll call back tomorrow	明日かけ直します
	ashita kakenaoshimasu
This is Mr.../Mrs...	...です
	...desu
How do I get an outside line?	外線はどうやって使いますか
	gaisen wa dooyatte tsukaimasu ka?

Communications

おつなぎしています otsunagi shite imasu	I'm trying to connect you
お話中です (o)hanashi-chuu desu	The line is engaged
またおかけ直しください mata okakenaoshi kudasai	Please try later
メッセージを残しますか messeeji o nokoshimasu ka?	Do you want to leave a message?
...アナウンスの後にメッセージを残してください ...anaunsu no ato ni messeeji o nokoshite kudasai	...leave a message after the tone

Please switch off all mobile phones	携帯電話の電源を切ってください keitai-denwa no dengen o kitte kudasai

Text messaging

SMS is not as popular in Japan as it is in some other countries, but sending emails to mobile phones is.

I will text you	メッセージを送ります
	messeeji o okurimasu
Can you text me?	私にメッセージを送ってもらえますか
	watashi ni messeeji o okutte moraemasu ka?

E-mail

New message:	新着メッセージ	shinchaku messeeji
To:	宛先	atesaki
From:	差出人	sashidashinin
Subject:	件名	kenmei
cc:	シーシー	shiishii
bcc:	ビーシーシー	biishiishii
Attachment:	添付	tempu
Send:	送信	sooshin

Do you have an e-mail?	Eメールがありますか
	iimeeru ga arimasu ka?
What is your e-mail address?	Eメールアドレスは何ですか
	iimeeru adoresu wa nan desu ka?
How do you spell it?	それはどう書きますか
	sore wa doo kakimasu ka?
All one word	一語です
	ichigo desu
All lower case	小文字です
	komoji desu
My e-mail address is...	私のEメールアドレスは ... です
	watashi no iimeeru adoresu wa ... desu
clare.smith @bit.co.uk	clare ドット smith アットマーク bit ドット co ドット uk
	shii eru ee aaru ii dotto esu emu ai ti eichi attomaaku bii ai tii dotto shii oo dotto yuu kei
Can I send an e-mail?	Eメールを送ることはできますか
	iimeeru o okuru koto wa dekimasu ka?
Did you get my e-mail?	私のEメールは届きましたか
	watashi no iimeeru wa todokimashita ka?

Internet

● ●

Computer and Internet terminology tends to be in English.

Are there any internet cafés here?	この辺りにインターネットカフェはありますか
	kono atari ni intaanetto kafe wa arimasu ka?
How much is it to log on for an hour?	１時間いくらですか
	ichi-jikan ikura desu ka?

Fax

. . . .

The international dialling code to send faxes to
Japan is **00 81** plus the Japanese area code without
the first **0**, for example, Tokyo **(0)33**, Osaka **(0)6**.

Addressing a fax
. . . .

宛　ate	to
より　yori	from
日付　hizuke	date
添付書類を見てください	please find attached
tempushorui o mite kudasai	
…のコピー　...no kopii	a copy of...
合計…ページです	...pages in total
gookei...peeji desu	

Do you have a fax?	ファックスがありますか
	fakkusu ga arimasu ka?
I want to send a fax	ファックスを送りたいです
	fakkusu o okuritai desu
What is your fax number?	ファックス番号は何番ですか
	fakkusu bangoo wa nan-ban desu ka?
My fax number is...	ファックス番号は …です
	fakkusu bangoo wa ... desu

Practicalities

Money

ATM's are usually open from 8.00 am until 11.00 pm, and for slightly shorter hours at the weekends. Most banks are only open from around 9.00 am to 3.00 pm (Monday to Friday). The yen is the currency of Japan. Japan still very much operates on cash and it can be problematic to find a place to use traveller's cheques and/or exchange currency. It is easier to change money at the airport or hotel.

クレジットカード kurejitto kaado	credit card
現金引き出し機/ATM genkin hikidashi ki/ee-tii-emu	cash dispenser
領収書　ryooshuusho	till receipt

Where can I change some money?	どこでお金を両替できますか
	doko de okane o ryoogae dekimasu ka?
When does the bank open?	いつ銀行は開きますか
	itsu ginkoo wa akimasu ka?
When does the bank close?	いつ銀行は閉まりますか
	itsu ginkoo wa simarimasu ka?
Can I pay with...?	...で払えますか
	...de haraemasu ka?
yen	円
	en
dollar	ドル
	doru
pound	ポンド
	pondo
I want to change these traveller's cheques	トラベラーズチェックを換金したいんですが
	toraberaazu chekku o kankin shitain desu ga
Where is the nearest cash dispenser?	最寄のATMはどこですか>?
	moyori no ee-tii-emu wa doko desu ka?

Can I use my credit card at the cash dispenser?	このATMで私のクレジットカードは使えますか
	kono ee-tii-emu de watashi no kurejitto kaado wa tsukaemasu ka?
Do you have any loose change?	小銭は持っていますか
	kozeni wa motte imasu ka?

Paying

How much is it?	いくらですか
	ikura desu ka?
How much will it be?	いくらになりますか
	ikura ni narimasu ka?
Can I pay by...?	...で払えますか
	...de haraemasu ka?
credit card	クレジットカード
	kurejitto kaado
cheque	チェック
	chekku
Is service included?	サービス料は含まれていますか
	saabisu-ryoo wa fukumarete imasu ka?
Is tax included?	税金は含まれていますか
	zeikin wa fukumarete imasu ka?

Put it on my bill	請求書に加えてください
	seikyuusho ni kuwaete kudasai
Where do I pay?	どこで支払いますか
	doko de siharaimasu ka?
I need a receipt, please	領収書をください
	ryooshuusho o kudasai
Do I pay in advance?	前払いですか
	maebarai desu ka?
Do I need to pay a deposit?	手付金は必要ですか
	tetsukekin wa hitsuyoo desu ka?
I'm sorry	すみません
	sumimasen
I've nothing smaller (no change)	細かいお金を持っていません
	komakai okane o motte imasen
	小銭がありません
	kozeni ga arimasen

YOU MAY HEAR...	
消費税込みです shoohizei komi desu	VAT is included
消費税は含まれていますが、 サービス料は別です shoohizei wa fukumarete imasu ga, saabisuryoo wa betsu desu	VAT is included but not a service charge

レジで支払ってください reji de siharatte kudasai	Pay at the till
最初に領収書/伝票をレ ジでもらってください saisho ni ryooshuusho/ dempyoo o reji de moratte kudasai	First get a receipt at the till (at airport, station bars, etc.)

Luggage

手荷物受取所 tenimotsu uketori-sho	baggage reclaim
携帯品一時預かり所 keitai-hin ichiji azukari-sho	left-luggage office
荷物用ワゴン nimotsu yoo wagon	luggage trolley

My luggage hasn't arrived	私の荷物が届いていません watashi no nimotsu ga todoite imasen

Practicalities

| My suitcase has been damaged on the flight | 私のスーツケースが飛行中に壊れてしまいました |
| | watashi no suutsukeesu ga hikoochuu ni kowarete shimaimashita |

Repairs

This is broken	これは壊れています
	kore wa kowarete imasu
Where can I have this repaired?	どこで修理できますか
	doko de shuuri dekimasu ka?
Is it worth repairing?	直す価値はありますか
	naosu kachi wa arimasu ka?
Can you repair...?	...は直せますか
	...wa naosemasu ka?
this	これ
	kore
these shoes	この靴
	kono kutsu
my watch	私の時計
	watashi no tokei

申し訳ありませんが、 直すことはできません mooshiwake arimasen ga, naosu koto wa dekimasen	Sorry, but we can't mend it

Laundry

ドライクリーニング dorai kuriiningu	dry-cleaner's
洗濯石鹸　sentaku sekken	soap powder
漂白剤　hyoohaku zai	bleach
洗濯機　sentakuki	washing machine

Where can I wash these clothes?	この衣類はどこで洗えますか kono irui wa doko de araemasu ka?
Where is the nearest launderette?	最寄のコインランドリーはど こですか moyori no koin randorii wa doko desu ka?

Practicalities

Complaints

· ·

The ... does/ do not work (for machines)	...が動きません ...ga ugokimasen
heating	暖房機 danbooki
air conditoning	エアコン eakon
The ... is/are dirty	...が汚れています ...ga yogorete imasu
toilet	トイレ toire
sheets	シーツ shiitsu
The light is not working	電気がつきません denki ga tsukimasen
It's broken	壊れています kowarete imasu
I want a refund	払い戻ししてください haraimodoshi shite kudasai

> **Hotel desk** (p 54)

Problems

Can you help me?	助けてもらえますか
	tasukete moraemasu ka?
I speak very little Japanese	私は少ししか日本語が話せません
	watashi wa sukoshi shika nihongo ga hanasemasen
Does anyone here speak English?	誰か英語が話せる人はいますか
	dareka eigo ga hanaseru hito wa imasu ka?
What's the matter?	どうしましたか
	doo shimashita ka?
I would like to speak to whoever is in charge of...	...の担当の方と話がしたいです
	...no tantoo no kata to hanashi ga shitai desu
I'm lost	道に迷いました
	michi ni mayoimashita
How do you get to...	...にはどう行けばいいですか
	...niwa doo ikeba ii desu ka
I missed my...	...に遅れてしまいました
	...ni okurete shimaimashita

train	電車
	densha
plane	飛行機
	hikooki
connection	乗り継ぎ
	noritsugi
I've missed my flight because there was an accident	事故があったので飛行機に乗り遅れてしまいました
	jiko ga atta node hikooki ni noriokurete shimaimashita
The coach has left without me	バスが出てしまいました
	basu ga dete shimaimashita
Can you show me how this works, please?	どうやって使うのかやってみせてもらえませんか
	dooyatte tsukau noka yatte misete moraemasen ka?
I have lost my money	お金をなくしてしまいました
	okane o nakushite shimaimashita
I need to get to...	...に行かなくてはいけないんです
	...ni ikanakutewa ikenain desu
I need to get in touch with the British consulate	英国領事館と連絡が取りたいです
	eikoku-ryoojikan to renraku ga toritai desu

Emergencies

医者	isha	doctor
救急車	kyuukyuusha	ambulance
警察	keisatsu	police
消防士	shoobooshi	firemen
消防署	shooboosho	fire station
警察署	keisatsu-sho	police station

Help!	助けて!
	tasukete!
Fire!	火事だ!
	kaji da!
Can you help me?	助けてもらえますか
	tasukete moraemasu ka?
There's been an accident!	事故があった!
	jiko ga atta!
Someone...	誰かが...
	dareka ga...
has been injured	怪我をしています
	kega o shite imasu
has been knocked down	倒れています
	taorete imasu
Please call...	...を呼んでください
	...o yonde kudasai

Where is the police station?	警察署はどこですか
	keisatsu-sho wa doko desu ka?
I want to report a crime	犯罪の報告がしたいです
	hanzai no hookoku ga shitai desu
I've been...	私は...
	watashi wa...
robbed	泥棒にあいました
	doroboo ni aimashita
attacked	襲われました
	osowaremashita
Someone's stolen...	誰かに ... を盗られました
	dareka ni ... o toraremashita
my bag	私のかばん
	watashi no kaban
traveller's cheques	トラベラーズチェック
	toraberaazu chekku
My car has been broken into	私の車が壊されました
	watashi no kuruma ga kowasaremashita
I've been raped	私は暴行を受けました
	watashi wa bookoo o ukemashita
I want to speak to a policewoman	女性の警察官と話がしたいです
	josei no keisatsukan to hanashi ga shitai desu

I need to make a telephone call	電話をかけなければいけません
	denwa o kakenakereba ikemasen
I need a report for my insurance	保険のための報告書をもらえますか
	hoken no tame no hookoku-sho o moraemasu ka
I didn't know there was a speed limit	制限速度があったのを知りませんでした
	seigen-sokudo ga atta no o shirimasen deshita
How much is the fine?	罰金はいくらですか
	bakkin wa ikura desu ka?
Where do I pay it?	どこで払いますか
	doko de haraimasu ka?
Do I have to pay it straightaway?	すぐに払わなければいけませんか
	suguni harawanakereba ikemasen ka?
I'm very sorry, officer	本当にすみませんでした
	hontoo ni sumimasen deshita

Health

Pharmacy

. . . .

A pharmacy can usually be found in major department stores and supermarkets.

薬局　yakkyoku	pharmacy/chemist

Can you give me something for...?	...に効く薬をもらえませんか
	...ni kiku kusuri o moraemasen ka?
a headache	頭痛
	zutsuu
car sickness	車酔い
	kuruma yoi
a cough	咳
	seki
diarrhoea	下痢
	geri
Is it safe for children?	これは子供にも安全ですか
	kore wa kodomo nimo anzen desu ka?

| How much should I give him? | どれだけ飲ませればいいですか |
| | doredake nomasereba ii desu ka? |

YOU MAY HEAR...

1日に3回... ichinichi ni sankai...	Three times a day...
...ご飯 ...gohan	...meals
食前 shokuzen	before meals
食中 shokuchuu	with meals
食後 shokugo	after meals

Body

In Japanese the possessive (my, his, her, etc.) is not generally used when refering to parts of the body, for example:

| I've broken <u>my</u> leg | **ashi** o otte shimaimashita |
| Mr Tanaka hurt <u>his</u> arm | Tanaka-san wa **ude** o itamete shimaimashita |

Doctor

• •

病院	byooin	**hospital**
救急	kyuukyuu	**emergency**

FACE TO FACE

具合が悪いです
guai ga warui desu
I feel ill

熱はありますか
netsu wa arimasu ka?
Do you have a temperature?

いいえ、...が痛みます
iie, ...ga itamimasu
No, I have a pain here...

I need a doctor	医者にかかりたいです
	isha ni kakaritai desu
My son is ill	息子が病気です
	musuko ga byooki desu
My daughter is ill	娘が病気です
	musume ga byooki desu
I'm diabetic	私は糖尿病です
	watashi wa toonyoobyoo desu

I'm pregnant	私は妊娠しています
	watashi wa ninshin shite imasu
I'm on the pill	私は薬を飲んでいます
	watashi wa kusuri o nonde imasu
I'm allergic to penicillin	ペニシリンのアレルギーがあります
	penishirin no arerugii ga arimasu
Will he/she have to go to hospital?	彼/彼女は病院に行かなければいけませんか
	kare/kanojo wa byooin ni ikanakereba ikemasen ka?
When are visiting hours?	診療時間はいつですか
	shinryoo-jikan wa itsu desu ka?
Will I have to pay?	支払わなければいけませんか
	shiharawanakereba ikemasen ka?
How much will it cost?	いくらかかりますか
	ikura kakarimasu ka?
Can you give me a receipt for the insurance?	保険のための領収書をもらえますか
	hoken no tame no ryooshuusho o moraemasu ka?

Health

> **Emergencies** (p 100)

あなたは病院に行かなければいけません anata wa byooin ni ikanakereba ikemasen	You will have to go to hospital
大したことはありません taishita koto wa arimasen	It's not serious

Dentist

. . . .

I need a dentist	歯医者にかかりたいです haisha ni kakaritai desu
I have a toothache	歯が痛いです ha ga itai desu
Can you do a temporary filling?	仮の詰め物はできますか kari no tsumemono wa dekimasu ka?
It hurts	痛いです itai desu
Can you give me something for the pain?	何か痛みに効く薬はありますか nanika itami ni kiku kusuri wa arimasu ka?

Can you repair my dentures?	義歯を治してもらえますか
	gishi o naoshite moraemasu ka?
Do I have to pay?	支払わなければいけませんか
	shiharawanakereba ikemasen ka?
How much will it be?	いくらかかりますか
	ikura kakarimasu ka?
Can I have a receipt for my insurance?	保険のための領収書をもらえますか
	hoken no tame no ryooshuusho o moraemasu ka?

YOU MAY HEAR...

抜かなければいけません	I'll have to take it out
nukanakereba ikemasen	
詰め物が必要です	You need a filling
tsumemono ga hitsuyoo desu	
少し痛むかもしれません	This might hurt a little
sukoshi itamu kamo shiremasen	

Health

> **Pharmacy** (p 103)

Different types of travellers

Disabled travellers

What facilities do you have for disabled people?	障害者用の設備はありますか shoogaisha-yoo no setsubi wa arimasu ka?
Are there any toilets for the disabled?	障害者用のトイレはありますか shoogaisha-yoo no toire wa arimasu ka?
Do you have any bedrooms on the ground floor?	一階の部屋がありますか ikkai no heya ga arimasu ka?
Is there a lift?	エレベーターはありますか erebeetaa wa arimasu ka?
Where is the lift?	エレベーターはどこにありますか erebeetaa wa doko ni arimasu ka?
Can you visit ... in a wheelchair?	...は車椅子でも行けますか ...wa kurumaisu demo ikemasu ka?

Do you have wheelchairs?	車椅子はありますか
	kurumaisu wa arimasu ka?
Where is the wheelchair-accessible entrance?	車椅子用の出入口はどこですか
	kurumaisu-yoo no deiriguchi wa doko desu ka?
Do you have an induction loop?	誘導ループシステムはありますか
	yuudoo ruupu shisutemu wa arimasu ka?
Is there a reduction for disabled people?	障害者割引はありますか
	shoogaisha waribiki wa arimasu ka?
Is there somewhere I can sit down?	どこか座れる所がありますか
	doko ka suwareru tokoro ga arimasu ka?

With kids

• •

Public transport is free for up to two non school children (normally) under 6 years old, when travelling with an adult. Children between the ages of 7 and 12 pay half price. Most tourist places give discounts to children and students.

> **Hotel desk** (p 54)

A child's ticket	子供の券
	kodomo no ken
This child is ... years old	この子は ... 歳です
	konoko wa ... sai desu
Is there a reduction for children?	子供割引はありますか
	kodomo waribiki wa arimasu ka?
Do you have a children's menu?	子供用メニューはありますか
	kodomo-yoo menyuu wa arimasu ka?
Is it OK to take children?	子供を連れて行ってもいいですか
	kodomo o tsurete itte mo ii desu ka?
Do you have...?	...はありますか
	...wa arimasu ka?
a high chair	子供用の椅子
	kodomo-yoo no isu
a cot	子供用のベッド
	kodomo-yoo no beddo
I have two children	私には子供が2人います
	watashi niwa kodomo ga futari imasu
This child is 8 years old	この子は8歳です
	konoko wa hassai desu
Do you have any children?	子供はいますか
	kodomo wa imasu ka?

With kids

> **Pharmacy** (p 103) > **Doctor** (p 105)

Reference

Measurements and quantities

●●●●●●●●●●●●●●●●●●●●●●●●●●●●●●●●●●●●

1 lb = approx. 0.5 kilo   1 pint = approx. 0.5 litre

Liquids

1/2 litre of...	...半リッター
a litre of...	...一リッター
a bottle of...	...一本
a glass of...	...一杯

1/2 litre of...   ...半リッター
...han-rittaa

a litre of...   ...一リッター
...ichi-rittaa

a bottle of...   ...一本
...ippon

a glass of...   ...一杯
...ippai

Weights

100 grams	百グラム hyaku-guramu
1/2 kilo of...	...五百グラム ...gohyaku-guramu
a kilo of...	...一キロ ...ichi-kiro

Food

a slice of...	...一切れ ...hito-kire
a portion of...	...一山 ...hito-yama
a dozen...	...一ダース ...ichi-daasu
a box of...	...一ケース ...hito-keesu
a packet of...	...一袋 ...hito-fukuro
a tin/a can of... (beer)	...一缶 ...hito-kan
a jar of...	...一瓶 ...hito-bin

Miscellaneous

...yen worth of...	...円相当の...
	...en sootoo no...
a quarter	四分の一
	yonbun no ichi
20 per cent	二十パーセント
	niju-paasento
more than...	...以上
	...ijoo
less than...	...以下
	...ika
double	二倍
	ni-bai
twice	二回
	ni-kai

Numbers

● ●

	Chinese-derived form		Original Japanese form
0	零	rei/zero	
1	一	ichi	hitotsu
2	二	ni	futatsu
3	三	san	mittsu
4	四	yon/shi	yottsu
5	五	go	itsutsu
6	六	roku	muttsu
7	七	shichi/nana	nanatsu
8	八	hachi	yattsu
9	九	kyuu/ku	kokonotsu
10	十	juu	too

Beyond ten, only the Chinese-derived form is used

11	十一	juu-ichi
12	十二	juu-ni
13	十三	juu-san
14	十四	juu-yon/shi
15	十五	juu-go
16	十六	juu-roku
17	十七	juu-shichi/nana

18	十八	juu-hachi
19	十九	juu-kyuu/ku
20	二十	nijuu
21	二十一	nijuu-ichi
22	二十二	nijuu-ni
23	二十三	nijuu-san
24	二十四	nijuu-yon/shi
25	二十五	nijuu-go
26	二十六	nijuu-rok
27	二十七	nijuu-shichi/nana
28	二十八	nijuu-hachi
29	二十九	nijuu-kyuu/ku
30	三十	san-juu
40	四十	yon-juu
50	五十	go-juu
60	六十	roku-juu
70	七十	sichi-juu/nana-juu
80	八十	hachi-juu
90	九十	kyuu-juu
100	百	hyaku
110	百十	hyaku-juu
1000	千	sen
2000	二千	ni-sen
10000	一万	ich-man
million	百万	hyaku-man
billion	十億	juuoku

1st	一つ目		6th	六つ目
	hitotsu-me			muttsu-me
2nd	二つ目		7th	七つ目
	futatsu-me			nanatsu-me
3rd	三つ目		8th	八つ目
	mittsu-me			yattsu-me
4th	四つ目		9th	九つ目
	yottsu-me			kokonotsu-me
5th	五つ目		10th	十番目
	itsutsu-me			juuban-me

Days and months

Days

Monday	月曜日	getsu-yoobi
Tuesday	火曜日	ka-yoobi
Wednesday	水曜日	sui-yoobi
Thursday	木曜日	moku-yoobi
Friday	金曜日	kin-yoobi
Saturday	土曜日	do-yoobi
Sunday	日曜日	nichi-yoobi

Months

January	一月	ichi-gatsu
February	二月	ni-gatsu
March	三月	san-gatsu
April	四月	shi-gatsu
May	五月	go-gatsu
June	六月	roku-gatsu
July	七月	shichi-gatsu
August	八月	hachi-gatsu
September	九月	ku-gatsu
October	十月	juu-gatsu
November	十一月	juuichi-gatsu
December	十二月	juuni-gatsu

Seasons

spring	春	haru
summer	夏	natsu
autumn	秋	aki
winter	冬	fuyu

What is today's date?	今日は何日ですか	kyoo wa nan-nichi desu ka?
What day is it today?	今日は何曜日ですか	kyoo wa nan-yoobi desu ka?

Reference

It's the 5th of March 2007	2007年の3月5日です
	nisen-nana nen no sangatsu itsuka desu
on Saturday	土曜日に
	do-yoobi ni
on Saturdays/ every Saturday	毎週土曜日に
	maishuu do-yoobi ni
this Saturday	今週の土曜日
	konshuu no do-yoobi ni
next Saturday	来週の土曜日
	raishuu no do-yoobi ni
last Saturday	先週の土曜日
	senshuu no do-yoobi ni
in June	6月に
	roku-gatsu ni
at the beginning of June	6月の初めに
	roku-gatsu no hajime ni
at the end of June	6月の終わりに
	roku-gatsu no owari ni
before summer	夏の前に
	natsu no mae ni
during the summer	夏中に
	natsujuu ni
after summer	夏の後に
	natsu no ato ni

Days and months

Time

••••••••••••••••••••••••••••••••

What time is it, please?	今、何時ですか
	ima nan-ji desu ka?
It's...	今...
	ima...
am	午前
	gozen
pm	午後
	gogo
2 o'clock	二時です
	ni-ji desu
3 o'clock	三時です
	san-ji desu
6 o'clock (etc.)	六時です
	roku-ji desu
It's 1 o'clock	今一時です
	ima ichi-ji desu
It's midday	今正午です
	ima shoogo desu
It's midnight	今は真夜中です
	ima wa mayonaka desu
9	九時
	ku-ji
9.10	九時十分
	ku-ji ju-ppun

quarter past 9	九時十五分 ku-ji juugo-fun
9.20	九時二十分 ku-ji niju-ppun
half past 9	九時半 ku-ji han
9.35	九時三十五分 ku-ji sanjuugo-fun
quarter to 10	十時十五分前 juu-ji juugo-fun mae
5 minutes to 10	十時五分前 juu-ji go-fun mae

Time phrases

When does it open?	いつ開きますか	itsu aki masu ka
When does it close?	いつ閉まりますか	itsu shimari masu ka
When does it begin?	いつ始まりますか	itsu hajimari masu ka
When does it finish?	いつ終わりますか	itsu owari masu ka
at 3 o'clock	三時に	san-ji ni
before 3 o'clock	三時前に	san-ji mae ni
after 3 o'clock	三時過ぎに	san-ji sugi ni
today	きょう	kyoo
tonight	今夜	konya
tomorrow	あした	ashita
yesterday	きのう	kinoo

Eating out

Food in Japan

All types of eating places and food can be found in Japan. Except for in hotel restaurants and up-market traditional Japanese restaurants which usually have set dining times, you can have your meal at any time throughout the day. American style fast food is popular and there are family restaurants that cater for this. There are also many specialized restaurants where only one type of food is served, for example, **Soba-ya** (Japanese noodle shop), **Raamen-ya** (Chinese noodle shop), **Sushi-ya** (Sushi restaurant), **Tonkatsu-ya** (pork cutlet restaurant) and even **Unagi** (BBQ eel restaurant). Visit **www.bento.com** for a guide to eating out in Japan.

Most coffee shops and restaurants will automatically bring you a glass of tap water (which is safe to drink) and **Oshibori**, a small hand towel to wipe your hands.

In traditional Japanese restaurants you will find low tables and (often) **tatami matting** which is a traditional Japanese mat made of straw. These restaurants require you to remove your shoes, so make sure your socks are respectable. Many eating places in Japan have plates of plastic food on display to show customers what they offer.

Service charge/Tax and tip

A consumer tax of 5% and a service charge of 10% are generally included in the bill and tipping is not customary.

Bill

The word for the bill is **(O)kanjoo**. You can ask for the bill by saying '(O)kanjoo onegai shimasu'.

Coffee shops 喫茶店 (kissaten)

Coffee shops serve non-alcoholic drinks and many of them also serve foods such as salads, sandwiches, pasta dishes and rice dishes. It is fun to find a good morning service which includes a small complementary breakfast when you order a coffee or tea. Ask for **mooningu setto**. If you would like to order tea with milk, be sure to specify **miruku tii**, as otherwise you will probably be served a lemon tea.

Noodle shops 蕎麦屋 (soba-ya)/うどん屋 (udon-ya) ラーメン屋 (raamen-ya)

Noodles are Japanese fast food. There are three popular types of noodles in Japan. These are **soba**, **udon** and **raamen**. **Soba** (buckwheat noodles) and **udon** (white flour noodles) are both traditional Japanese noodles. You can choose different toppings such as chicken or tempura. **Raamen** originated from China but has gained huge popularity amongst all generations in Japan. It comes in hot soup or is served cold without soup, in summer.

Sushi shops 鮨屋 (sushi-ya)

There are a number of different **sushi** types but the most popular are **nigiri-zushi**, (a rice ball shaped in the palm of the hand with raw fish on top), and **temaki-zushi**, (rice and raw fish often wrapped in a cone shape with a seaweed sheet wrapper). **Toro**, a special part of tuna, is also very popular. Although generally **sushi** is expensive, you can find good deals at lunch time or at very cheap and decent quality 'rotating' (kaiten) sushi shops where you can see the sushi and pick what you fancy. One plate usually costs only 100 yen.

Tempura shops 天麩羅屋 (tempura-ya)

Tempura is a deep fried dish of vegetables and seafood in light batter. It was originally introduced by the Portuguese. Some shops prepare **tempura** in front of you and serve it in a very elegant manner.

Pubs 居酒屋 (izaka-ya)

Izaka-ya are very good places to try out a range of Japanese food and drink. They serve cheap but very tasty food in small portions similar to Spanish tapas, and usually have a large selection to choose from. Amongst these, **Yakitori** (BBQ chicken), **Agedashi-dofu** (deep-fried bean curd) and **Sashimi** (sliced raw fish) are all worth trying.

Family restaurants
ファミリーレストラン (famirii resutoran)

There are many chain family restaurants where you can have different types of food. They are often located on major roads.

Vending machines 自動販売機 (jidoo-hanbaiki)

Vending machines contain all kinds of hot and cold drinks as well as snacks. Notes can be used in the machines.

Convenience stores コンビニ (konbini)

If you need a late-night snack or don't want to go to a restaurant, a convenience store is a good place to stock up on snacks. Sandwiches, salads, pot noodles, etc. are all available to buy, as well as rice balls, which have various fillings and can become addictive.

Department stores デパート (depaato)

Most department stores have a designated restaurant floor (usually on the top floor) where you will find various types of restaurant, including western style. These are good places to visit to familiarize yourself with the kind of food you can get in Japan.

Department store basement floors have good delis and take-away food.

Lunch boxes お弁当 (obentoo)

Obentoo is a pre-packed lunchbox. You can buy various types from department stores, convenience stores, supermarkets and even train stations. Each train station sells specialized lunchboxes prepared with local delicacies such as dimsum lunchbox in Yokohama, Tempura riceball in Nagoya, BBQ eel in Hamamatsu and Trout sushi in Toyama.

FACE TO FACE

A ご注文は?
gochuumon wa?
May I have your order?

B ミルクティーをお願いします
miruku tii o onegai shimasu
A tea with milk, please

a coffee	コーヒー	
	koohii	
a lager	ビール	
	biiru	
a lemon squash	レモンスカッシュ	
	remon sukasshu	
with lemon	レモンで	
	remon de	

no sugar	砂糖なしで
	satoo nashi de
for two	二人に
	futari ni
for me	私に
	watashi ni
for him/her	彼/彼女に
	kare/kanojo ni
for us	私たちに
	watashitachi ni
with ice	氷を入れて
	koori o irete
a bottle of	ミネラルウォーター一本
mineral water	mineraru wootaa ippon
sparkling	炭酸水
	tansansui
still	ミネラルウォーター
	mineraru wootaa

Other drinks to try

Iced coffee アイスコーヒー aisukoohii is very
    popular in Japan.

Japanese tea お茶 ocha is usually served with your
    meal for free in Japanese restaurants including
    Japanese noodle shops. You can buy chilled or hot
    canned tea from vending machines. There are
    many kinds to choose from.

Green tea 抹茶 maccha/グリーンティー guriin tii
   is the tea used at tea ceremonies and is rather
   bitter, but a sweet iced green tea is available in
   some coffee shops. Green tea ice cream is a
   popular favourite.

Japanese rice wine 酒 sake can be drunk either
   chilled or warmed. There are different degrees of
   sweetness and lots of local ones, which are called
   地酒 jizake.

焼酎 Shoochuu is Japanese vodka. It is cheap and
   again there are many local varieties.

チュウハイ Chuuhai is a mixture of shoochuu and
   lemonade, etc. which is popular among young
   people.

梅酒 Umeshu is Japanese plum wine. It is smooth
   and sweet and many women are fond of it.

Reading the menu

Although traditional Japanese cuisine, **kaiseki-ryoori**, has a long list of dishes (which is usually a set course), most Japanese restaurants, unlike western restaurants, do not have starters or main meals. Below are sample menus for some of the popular eating places.

General Japanese restaurant

Food/Drink: please refer to the **Izakaya** section below. They often have a set meal (定食 teishoku), which is a main dish with a bowl of rice, soup, and a side dish all served together on a tray.

Table top cooking restaurant

鉄板焼き teppan-yaki meat, seafood and vegetables cooked on a table-top hot plate

すき焼き suki-yaki sliced beef, bean curd, mushroom and other vegetables cooked in a soy sauce based sauce

しゃぶしゃぶ shabu-shabu thinly sliced beef dipped and cooked quickly in a hot stock, eaten with sesame seed, soy sauce and Japanese lime based dip

Izakaya

Food: normally served in a small portions

Beef 牛肉 (gyuu-niku)

牛丼 gyuu-don sliced beef cooked with soy sauce on rice

牛肉たたき gyuu-niku tataki seared sliced beef
  served with ginger
牛刺し gyuu-sashi sliced raw beef
ハンバーグ hambaagu hamburger steak
ハンバーガー hambaagaa hamburger
串かつ kushi-katsu crumbed meat and vegetables,
  deep-fried on skewers
肉じゃが nikujaga sliced beef cooked with potato in
  a soy sauce based stock
レバー rebaa grilled or pan-fried liver
しゃぶしゃぶ shabushabu thinly sliced beef
  cooked quickly at the table in boiling stock
すきやき suki-yaki sliced beef with vegetables and
  raw egg, cooked at the table
ステーキ suteeki steak
焼き肉 yaki-niku grilled sliced beef

Chicken 鶏肉 (tori-niku)

から揚げ karaage deep-fried chicken coated in
  mild spice and herbs
ねぎま negima char-grilled skewered chicken and
  spring onion
竜田揚げ tatta-age deep-fried marinated (soy
  sauce, sake, ginger) chicken
照り焼きチキン teriyaki-chikin pan-fried chicken in
  teriyaki-sauce (soy sauce and rice wine)

つくね tsukune minced chicken ball char-grilled
   and coated with soy sauce
焼き鳥 yaki-tori char-grilled skewered chicken

Pork 豚肉 (buta-niku)

豚肉の生姜焼き buta-niku no shooga yaki pan-fried
   thinly sliced pork with soy sauce and ginger
餃子 gyooza fried pork dumpling
かつ丼 katsudon deep-fried, bread-crumbed pork
   cutlet on rice
かつカレー katsu-karee deep-fried, bread-crumbed
   pork and curry on rice
とんかつ tonkatsu deep-fried, bread-crumbed pork
   cutlet
焼き豚/チャーシュー yakibuta/chaashuu sliced
   roast pork

Fish 魚 (sakana) and other seafood dishes

See type of fish in the Sushi shop section below.

刺身 sashimi sliced raw fish
焼き魚 yaki-zakana grilled fish
煮魚 ni-zakana simmered fish
エビフライ ebi-furai deep-fried, crumbed prawn
えび天ぷら ebi-tempura deep-fried prawn in light
   batter topped on rice

かきフライ kaki-furai deep-fried, crumbed oyster

かにすき kanisuki hotpot dish with crabs

かに酢 (の物) kanisu (nomono) crab meat in white rice vinegar

かつおたたき katsuo tataki seared bonito with grated ginger

いかの姿焼き ika no sugata-yaki whole grilled squid

いわしの生姜煮 iwashi no shooga-ni simmered gingered sardine

さばの塩焼き saba no shioyaki salt-grilled mackerel

さばの味噌煮 saba no misoni simmered mackerel in miso sauce

さばの竜田揚げ saba no tatta-age deep-fried marinated (soy sauce, sake, ginger) mackerel

さんまの塩焼き samma no shioyaki salt-grilled (Pacific) saury

酢牡蛎 sugaki fresh oyster in vinegar

刺身盛り合わせ sashimi moriawase assorted sliced raw fish

たこ焼き takoyaki octopus cooked in a dough ball

たら tara cod

たらの味噌焼き tara no miso yaki grilled cod with soy bean paste

てっさ tessa thinly sliced raw puffer fish (prepared by a licensed chef)

うな重 unajuu/うな丼 unadon grilled eel on rice

Vegetables 野菜 (yasai)

揚げだし豆腐 agedashi-doofu deep-fried bean curd

だし巻き卵 dashimaki tamago rolled flavoured eggs

ふろふきだいこん furoruki daikon simmered
Japanese radish with sauce

冷奴 hiyayakko cold bean curd

ほうれん草おひたし hoorensoo ohitashi cooked
spinach with sesame seeds

かぼちゃの煮物 kabocha no nimono simmered
pumpkin

きんぴらごぼう kimpira goboo shaved burdock
root, pan-fried with soy sauce and chilli

きのこ kinoko various mushrooms

こんにゃく konnyaku hard, jelly like product made
from root vegetables

きゅうりの酢の物 kyuuri no suno mono sliced
cucumber in vinegar

のり nori dried seaweed sheet

納豆 nattoo fermented soy beans

ポテトフライ poteto furai chips

白和え shiraae boiled vegetables mixed with bean
curd

漬物 tsukemono pickled vegetables

わかめの酢の物 wakame no suno mono seaweed in
vinegar

焼きなす yakinasu grilled aubergine

焼きしいたけ yaki-shiitake grilled Japanese
   shiitake-mushroom
野菜天ぷら yasai tempura deep-fried vegetables in
   light batter

Rice ご飯 (gohan) and others

おでん oden various vegetables, bean curd and
   skewered beef tendon cooked in stock
お好み焼き okonomi-yaki Japanese style pizza
   (see more in **Okonomi-yaki** shop section)
そば soba thin, brown, buckwheat noodles
   (see more in noodle shop section)
うどん udon thick, white, wheat flour noodles
   (see more in noodle shop section)
ラーメン raamen Chinese style noodles
   (see more in noodle shop section)
カレー karee curry and rice
かつカレー katsu-karee bread-crumbed, deep-fried
   pork on curry and rice
かつ丼 katsu-don crumbed, deep-fried pork, egg
   and onion cooked with soy sauce on rice
天丼 tendon deep-fried prawn in light batter on rice
牛丼 gyuudon sliced beef, onion and egg cooked
   with soy sauce on rice
スパゲティー supagetii spaghetti
ピザ piza pizza

雑炊 zoosui Japanese savoury rice porridge with egg

鮭茶漬け sake-chazuke Japanese tea poured over
    rice, flaked salmon and seaweed

お茶漬け o-chazuke Japanese tea poured over rice

おにぎり onigiri rice ball wrapped with seaweed
    sheet

焼き飯 yakimeshi Japanese style fried rice

チャーハン chaahan Chinese style fried rice

Soup 汁 (shiru)

豆腐の味噌汁 toofu no misoshiru soy bean paste
    based soup with soy bean curd

わかめの味噌汁 wakame no misoshiru soy bean
    paste based soup with seaweed

ねぎの味噌汁 negi no misoshiru soy bean paste
    based soup with spring onion

あげの味噌汁 age no misoshiru soy bean paste
    based soup with bean curd sheet

雑煮 zooni soup with rice cake

すまし汁 sumashijiru clear soup

Drinks お飲み物 (o-nomimono)

ビール biiru lager beer

生ビール nama biiru draft beer

大瓶 oo-bin large bottle of lager

小瓶 ko-bin small bottle of lager
大ジョッキ dai-jokki large glass of lager
中ジョッキ chuu-jokki medium glass of lager
小ジョッキ shoo-jokki small glass of lager
酒 sake Japanese rice wine, warm or chilled
チュウハイ chuuhai Japanese vodka with
  lemonade
水割り mizu-wari whisky with water
コーラ koora cola
ジュース juusu juice
オレンジジュース orenji-juusu orange juice
お茶 o-cha Japanese tea. Traditionally in a sushi
  shop, tea is served after you finish the meal.
  This tea is called あがり agari.
水 mizu water
炭酸水 tansansui sparkling water
ミネラルウォーター mineraru wootaa mineral
  water (still)
コーヒー koohii coffee
紅茶 koocha English tea

Sushi shop

Sushi: normally means rice balls (**nigiri**) with sliced
raw fish but there are various types.

にぎり(鮨) nigiri (zushi) rice balls with sliced raw fish

手巻き寿司 temaki-zushi rolled sushi with seaweed
  sheet (without using bamboo sheet)
巻き寿司 maki-zushi rolled sushi with seaweed
  sheet using bamboo sheet
細巻き hoso-maki small rolled sushi
太巻き futo-maki large rolled sushi with cooked
  egg, vegetable, mushroom, etc. usually vegetarian
いなり寿司 inari-zushi seasoned rice, wrapped in
  fried thin bean curd
カッパ (巻き) kappa (maki) small rolled sushi with
  cucumber
盛り合わせ moriawase assorted sushi

For **nigiri** and **temaki**, you can choose what to put
on/in from below:

あまえび amaebi sweet shrimps
赤貝 akagai ark shell (red shellfish)
穴子 anago conger eel (usually grilled)
あわび awabi abalone
えび ebi prawn
貝 kai shellfish
かに kani crab
かつお katsuo bonito
ひらめ hirame plaice
ホタテ hotate scallop
いか ika squid
いくら ikura salmon roe

139

いわし iwashi sardine
まぐろ maguro tuna
さば saba mackerel
鯛 tai snapper
たこ tako octopus
うなぎ unagi eel (usually grilled)
うに uni sea urchin
卵 tamago sliced, flavoured egg omelette

Soup and others

味噌汁 misoshiru soy bean paste based soup
すまし汁 sumashi-jiru clear soup
茶碗蒸し chawan-mushi steamed flavoured egg
  with vegetable, chicken, mushroom and prawn
わさび wasabi Japanese green horseradish
がり gari thinly sliced, pickled ginger

Drinks: お飲み物 o-nomimono (See the **Izakaya**
section).

Noodle shop

そば soba thin, brown, buckwheat noodles
うどん udon thick, white, wheat flour noodles
そうめん soo-men thin, white, wheat flour cold
  noodles
ラーメン raamen Chinese style noodles

Udon and Soba

釜揚げうどん kamaage udon warm/cold udon with dipping sauce

カレーうどん/そば karee udon/soba udon/soba in curry soup

きつねうどん kitsune udon udon with flavoured bean curd sheet

木の葉うどん/そば konoha udon/soba udon/soba in soup with sliced fish paste

鍋焼きうどん nabeyaki udon udon cooked in a clay pot with vegetables, chicken, prawn, etc.

肉うどん/そば niku udon/soba udon/soba in soup with sliced beef

山菜うどん/そば sansai udon/soba udon/soba in soup with wild vegetables

たぬきうどん/そば tanuki udon/soba udon/soba in soup with deep-fried light batter

天ぷらうどん/そば tempura udon/soba udon/soba in soup with deep-fried prawn in light batter

天ざる tenzaru cold soba and deep-fried prawn in light batter with dipping sauce

ニシンそば nishin soba soba in soup with smoked herring

わかめうどん/そば wakame udon/soba udon/soba in soup with seaweed

ざるそば zaru soba cold soba with dipping sauce

Raamen: use chilli powder for **miso raamen** but pepper (**koshoo**) for others.

味噌ラーメン miso raamen raamen in soy bean paste based soup
塩ラーメン shio raamen raamen in salt based soup
醤油ラーメン shooyu raamen raamen in soy sauce based soup
チャーシュー chaashuu raamen in soy sauce based soup with an extra topping of sliced roast pork
チャンポン麺 champon-men raamen in pork stock based soup with stir-fry meat and vegetables
コーンラーメン koon raamen raamen with sweet cone
もやしラーメン moyashi raamen raamen with extra bean sprout topping
とんこつラーメン tonkotsu raamen raamen in pork stock based soup

Rice dishes and others

チャーハン chaahan Chinese style fried rice
えび天丼 ebi-tendon deep-fried prawn in light batter on rice
いなり寿司 inari-zushi seasoned rice, wrapped in fried thin bean curd

カレーライス karee raisu curry with rice

おにぎり onigiri rice ball wrapped with seaweed
sheet

親子丼 oyako-don (buri) chicken and egg topped on
rice

天ぷら tempura deep-fried seafood and vegetables
in light batter

天丼 tendon deep-fried vegetables and prawn in
light batter topped on rice

うどん/そば定食 udon/soba teishoku set meal with
udon/soba, rice and side dish

焼き飯 yaki-meshi Japanese style fried rice

焼きうどん/そば yaki udon/soba udon/soba stir-
fry with meat and vegetables

餃子 gyooza fried pork dumpling

Drinks: お飲み物 o-nomimono (See the **Izakaya**
section).

Okonomi-yaki shop

お好み焼き okonomi-yaki Japanese style pizza,
sliced cabbage and meat or seafood cooked in soft
dough on a hot plate

焼きそば yakisoba stir-fried Chinese noodles with
meat and vegetables

焼きうどん yakiudon stir-fried thick white flour
   noodles with meat and vegetables
モダン焼き modan-yaki yakisoba in thin flour crêpe
広島焼き Hiroshima-yaki Hiroshima style,
   ingredients covered with a thin flour crêpe instead
   of mixing them with dough
おにぎり onigiri rice ball

You can choose what to put in from the following:

牛肉 gyuu-niku beef
豚肉 buta-niku pork
えび ebi shrimps
いか ika squid
たこ tako octopus
野菜 yasai vegetables (yasai-yaki is without any
   meat/seafood)
ねぎ negi spring onion (negi-yaki uses spring onion
   instead of cabbage)
卵/玉子 tamago egg

Drinks: お飲み物 o-nomimono (See the **Izakaya**
section)

FACE TO FACE

A ...人分席を予約したいんですが
...nin bun seki o yoyaku shitain desu ga
I'd like to book a table for ... people

B はい、いつですか
hai, itsu desu ka?
Yes, when for?

A 今夜.../明日の夜.../八時に
konya.../asu no yoru.../hachi-ji ni
for tonight/for tomorrow night/at 8 o'clock

The menu, please	メニュー、ください
	menyuu, kudasai
What is the dish of the day?	今日のお薦めは何ですか
	kyoo no osusume wa nan desu ka?
Do you have a tourist menu?	旅行者用のメニューはありますか
	ryokoosha-yoo no menyuu wa arimasu ka?
at a set price?	セットの値段ですか
	setto no nedan desu ka?
What is the speciality of the house?	ここのお薦めは何ですか
	koko no osusume wa nan desu ka?
Can you tell me what this is?	これは何ですか
	kore wa nan desu ka?

I'll have this	これ、お願いします
	kore, onegai shimasu
Could we have some more ..., please?	もう少し ...、をもらえますか
	moo sukoshi ..., o moraemasu ka
bread	パン
	pan
water	水
	mizu
The bill, please	お勘定、お願いします
	okanjoo, onegai shimasu
Is service included?	サービス料は含まれていますか
	saabisuryoo wa fukumarete imasu ka?

Vegetarian

The majority of restaurants do not indicate vegetarian food but there are always some vegetarian dishes on the menu. Don't hesitate to tell the staff that you are a vegetarian and what you can and cannot eat; they will be happy to advise you on suitable dishes.

I am a vegetarian	私はベジタリアンです
	watashi wa bejitarian desu
I don't eat meat	肉を食べません
	niku o tabemasen
I don't eat meat and fish	肉と魚を食べません
	niku to sakana o tabemasen
Do you have any vegetarian dishes?	野菜だけの料理はありますか
	yasai dake no ryoori wa arimasu ka?
Which dishes have no...?	...が入っていない料理はどれですか
	...ga haitte inai ryoori wa dore desu ka?
meat	肉
	niku
fish?	魚
	sakana
What fish dishes do you have?	どんな魚料理がありますか
	donna sakana ryoori ga arimasu ka?
What do you recommend?	何かお薦めはありますか
	nanika osusume wa arimasu ka?
I don't like meat	(お)肉が嫌いです
	(o-)niku ga kirai desu
Egg is all right	卵は大丈夫です
	tamago wa daijoobu desu

| Is it made with vegetable or seaweed stock? | これは野菜かこぶだしで作られていますか？ |
| | kore wa yasai ka kobu dashi de tsukurarete imasu ka? |

Possible dishes

山菜料理 sansai ryoori Japanese vegetarian dish which could be a full course meal.

おひたし ohitashi Japanese salad (steamed spinach or beans, etc. with sesame seeds)

味噌汁 misoshiru Japanese soup

豆腐 toofu bean curd (very popular)

冷奴 hiyayakko chilled tofu

揚げだし豆腐 agedashi doofu deep-fried tofu

卵丼 tamago domburi rice with cooked egg and vegetables (onions) in a soy sauce based sauce

揚げだし卵 agedashi tamago Japanese omelette

巻き寿司 maki-zushi rolled sushi with mixed ingredients which are usually vegetarian. You can also try カッパ巻き kappamaki (cucumber rolls) or 卵巻き tamagomaki (egg rolls)

山菜うどん/蕎麦 sansai udon/soba udon (white Japanese flour based noodles) or soba (dark coloured buckwheat noodles) in soup with vegetables

わかめうどん/蕎麦 wakame udon/soba served
with seaweed

ざるそば zaru soba chilled soba with dipping sauce

野菜お好み焼き yasai okonomiyaki Japanese style
pizza with sliced cabbage, spring onion and egg,
prepared on a hot plate

野菜天ぷら yasai tempura deep-fried vegetables in
light batter

きのこスパゲティー kinoko supagetii	spaghetti with various Japanese mushrooms
野菜 yasai	vegetable(s)
山菜 sansai	edible wild plants

Wines and spirits

The wine list, please	ワインメニューを見せてくだ さい
	wain menyuu o misete kudasai
white wine	白ワイン
	shiro wain
red wine	赤ワイン
	aka wain
Can you recommend a good local wine?	地元名産のいいワインはあり ますか
	jimoto meisan no ii wain wa arimasu ka?
Can you recommend a good local sake?	地元名産のいいお酒はありま すか
	jimoto meisan no ii osake wa arimasu ka?
A bottle of...	...を一本
	...o ippon
house wine	ハウスワイン
	hausu wain
What liqueurs do you have?	どんなお酒がありますか
	donna osake ga arimasu ka?

Grammar

Introduction
• •

This is a guide to some of the basic concepts and
rules in Japanese. It is designed to enable you to
form simple sentences. There are different levels
of politeness in Japanese but polite forms, suitable
for travellers to use without being rude, have been
used throughout this book, including the dictionary
section.

Although writing is rather complicated, Japanese
grammar is simple compared to that of most
European languages. For example, there is no
gender; there are no plural forms; and verbs only
have past and non-past (present) forms.

Sentence structure

The basic Japanese sentence has a topic and
a comment section. The topic (which is indicated
by a topic marker '**wa**') usually comes at the
beginning of the sentence, but if the topic is
understood among the speakers, it is often omitted.

(Watashi wa) Yamashita desu. (I) am Yamashita.

Grammar

Particles

Japanese contains particles similar to English
prepositions but in Japanese they come after the
words. Particles have the following functions.

wa topic marker
ga subject marker
ka question marker
o   direct object marker
ni in-direct object marker, goal and position
        marker
to means 'and' (connect words)
de indicates means

Word order

Japanese word order is: subject – object – verb. Therefore, 'I eat Sushi' becomes '**I Sushi eat**'; **Watashi wa Sushi o tabemasu**. When the comment part is long, for example, 'I will eat Sushi with my friend in London tomorrow', as long as you put **I** (which is the topic) and **will eat**, (which is the verb) in their respective places and you move the object together with the necessary particle, the words can be in any order.

Questions and negatives

Polite Japanese verbs end with **masu** and a sentence containing nouns and adjectives end with **desu**.

You can create a question by simply adding the question marker '**ka**' at the end of the sentence.

This is Tokyo	Tokyo desu
Is it Tokyo?	Tokyo desu **ka**?

Negative sentences can be made by changing the ending of the predicate such as verb or adjective accordingly.

non-past positive	non-past negative	past positive	past negative
-desu	-dewa arimasen	-deshita	-dewa arimasen deshita
-masu	-masen	-mashita	-masen deshita

I eat Sushi.	Sushi o tabe-**masu**
I don't eat Sushi	Sushi o tabe-**masen**
I ate Sushi	Sushi o tabe-**mashita**
I didn't eat Sushi	Sushi o tabe-**masendeshita**

It is quiet	Shizuka **desu**
It is not quiet	Shizuka **dewa arimasen**
It was quiet	Shizuka **deshita**
It was not quiet	Shizuka **dewa arimasen deshita**

Expressing desire

Change masu to **taidesu**, for example, tabe-masu to **tabe-taidesu**, 'I would like to eat', and nomi-masu to **nomi-taidesu**, 'I would like to drink'.

Verb forms 1

The verbs can be divided into two groups.

The first group is verbs ending in '**e**', such as tabe-masu (eat) and age-masu (give). This group also includes the verbs with one syllable (see pronunciation section) before masu such as mi-masu (watch), ki-masu (come/put on). A few exceptional verbs belonging to this group include; oki-masu (get up) and ori-masu (get off).

The second group is verbs ending in '**i**', such as nomi-masu (drink) and kai-masu (buy).

In order to make a request or ask permission, you need to know how to make the so called te-form of the verbs. For the verbs in the first group, you can simply replace 'masu' with 'te' tabe-te, age-te, mi-te and ki-te. However, for the second group, you have to pay attention to which syllable comes before 'masu'.

syllable before 'masu'	change to	verbs e.g.	te-form
shi	shite (no change)	hana**shi**-masu (talk)	hana**shite**
i, chi, ri	tte	ka**i**-masu (buy)	ka**tte**
ki, gi, ji	ite	ki**ki**-masu (listen/ask)	ki**ite**
mi, ni, bi,	nde	yo**mi**-masu (read)	yo**nde**

Making a request

If you would like someone to provide you with something, you can use the words kudasai (please give me) or onegaishimasu (please). For example, **Reshiito o kudasai**, 'Can I have a receipt please', or **Reshiito, onegaishimau**, 'receipt please'.

If you want something to be done, use the verb te-form then add **kudasai** at the end: for example, 'please speak', **hanashite kudasai**; 'please buy', **katte kudasai**; 'please eat', **tabete kudasai**.

Asking permission

Use the verb te-form and add **mo ii desu ka**. Is it all right to eat? **Tabete mo ii desu ka**. Is it all right to take a photo? **Shashin o totte mo ii desu ka**. (shashin: photo(s), o: object marker, totte: te-form of verb torimasu, take)

Asking possibility/ability

Use the noun plus **dekimasu ka**. For example, 'Can we park here?' **Koko ni chuusha dekimasu ka** 'Can we hold a meeting?' **Miitingu ga dekimasu ka** 'Can we eat here?' **Koko de shokuji ga dekimasu ka**

However, if you would like to use verbs, you must remember the two groups (see above).

For verbs in the first group, you simply change
-masu to -raremasu, then add the question marker
ka at the end for the first group. So, if you would like
to say, Can we eat here?, it would be **Koko de tabe-
raremasu ka**, and Can we watch TV here? would be
Koko de terebi ga mi-raremasu ka.

For verbs in the second group, you need to change
the vowel **i** in the syllable before masu to **e** as
shown below.

verbs e.g.	change to	English	Japanese
i**ki**-masu (go)	i**ke**-masu (can go)	Can we go to Tokyo?	Tokyoo ni ike-masu ka?
ka**i**-masu (buy)	ka**e**-masu (can buy)	Can we buy it?	Sore ga kae-masu ka?
ki**ki**-masu (listen/ask)	ki**ke**-masu (can listen/ask)	Can we listen to the radio?	Rajio ga kike-masu ka?
yo**mi**-masu (read)	yo**me**-masu (can read)	Can we read the papers?	Shimbun ga yome-masuka?

Magic word

Sumimasen; excuse me or sorry, is a magic word in Japanese and similar to how please is used in English. As long as you use this word, especially when you are making a request, asking permission, or trying to get someone's attention, you will be fine.

Grammar

Public holidays

Most shops and offices are closed on the first three days in January. Department stores are very busy with people buying presents at the end of the year and mid-summer. Although **Obon** (13-16 August), which is similar to Christmas, is not a National holiday, many people take holidays and go back to their hometown so the roads and public transport become extremely busy.

Similarly, during the so called Golden week holiday (end of April to the beginning of May) it is extremely busy with Japanese people travelling. Make sure you have reservations in advance if you are planning to travel during these periods.

National holidays in Japan

January 1	元日	ganjitsu	New Year's Day
2nd Monday in January	成人の日	seijin no hi	Coming of Age Day
February 11	建国記念日	kenkoku kinen-bi	National Foundation Day
Equinox Day (around 21 March)	春分の日	shumbun no hi	Vernal Equinox Day

April 29	昭和の日 shoowa no hi	
	Showa Day	
May 3	憲法記念日 kempoo kinen-bi	
	Constitution Memorial Day	
May 4	みどりの日 midori no hi	
	Greenery Day	
May 5	こどもの日 kodomo no hi	
	Children's Day	
3rd Monday in July	海の日 umi no hi Marine Day	
3rd Monday in September	敬老の日 keiroo no hi	
	Respect for the Aged Day	
Equinox Day (around 23 September)	秋分の日 shuubun no hi	
	Autumnal Equinox Day	
2nd Monday in October	体育の日 taiiku no hi	
	Health and Sports Day	
November 3	文化の日 bunka no hi	
	National Cultural Day	
November 23	勤労感謝の日 kinroo kansha no hi Labour Thanksgiving Day	
December 23	天皇誕生日 tennoo tanjoo-bi	
	Emperor's Birthday	

If the national holiday falls on a Sunday, the following closest non-holiday day becomes the substitute holiday.

Signs and notices

Airport/station

Most signs in airports and large stations are bilingual, but local stations have little in English so the following guides will be useful.

駅	eki	station
地下鉄	chikatetsu	metro
入口	iriguchi	entrance
出口	deguchi	exit
改札口	kaisatsu guchi	ticketing gate
中央改札口	chuuoo kaisatsu guchi	main gate
南口	minami guchi	south gate
西口	nishi guchi	west gate
北口	kita guchi	north gate
東口	higashi guchi	east gate
非常口	hijoo guchi	emergency exit
みどりの窓口	midori no madoguchi	JR ticketing counter

切符	kippu	ticket
JRパス	jei aaru pasu	JR pass
パスポート	pasupooto	passport
引換券	hikikaeken	voucher/coupon
売り場	uriba	sales section
本日中	honjitsuchuu	today's
在来線	zairaisen	local lines
子供	kodomo	children
大人	otona	adult
円	en	yen
入場料	nyuujooryoo	entrance charge

Inside the station

...番線	...bansen	platform...
プラットホーム	purattohoomu	platform
エスカレーター	esukareetaa	escalator
エレベーター	erebeetaa	lift
階段	kaidan	stairs
車椅子	kurumaisu	wheelchair
昇り / 上り	nobori	going up
下り	kudari	going down

On the platform

●●●●●●●●●●●●●●●●●●●●●●●●●●●●●●●●●●●●●●●

...行き	...iki	bound for...
...発	...hatsu	depart...
...着	...chaku	arrive...
普通	futsuu	standard
急行	kyuukoo	rapid
特急	tokkyuu	super rapid
新幹線	shinkansen	bullet train
この電車	kono densha	this train
次	tsugi	next
先	saki	before
後	ato	later
通過	tsuuka	pass
停車	teisha	stop
グリーン車	guriin-sha	first class
指定席	shiteiseki	reserved
自由席	jiyuuseki	non-reserved
寝台車	shindai-sha	sleeping car
...線	...sen	line...
乗り換え	norikae	to change (buses/trains)
遅れ	okure	delay
事故	jiko	accident

Vending machine/telephone

●●●●●●●●●●●●●●●●●●●●●●●●●●●●●●●●●●●●

自動販売機	jidoo hambaiki	vending machine
水	mizu	water
お茶	ocha	Japanese tea
両替	ryoogae	money exchange
売り切れ	urikire	out of stock
故障	koshoo	out of order
つり銭切れ	tsurisengire	out of change
お釣り	otsuri	change
キオスク	kiosuku	kiosk
電話	denwa	telephone
国際	kokusai	international
国内	kokunai	national
カード	kaado	card
押す	osu	push
引く	hiku	pull

In the carriage

●●

開	kai	open
閉	hei	close
自動ドア・扉	jidoo doa/tobira	automatic door/ door
禁煙	kinen	non-smoking
喫煙	kitsuen	smoking
喫煙所/喫煙室	kitsuen-jo/ -shitsu	smoking area/ room
マナーモード	manaa moodo	silent mode
食堂車	shokudoo-sha	dining car
ビュッフェ	byuffe	buffet
機内/車内販売	kinai/shanai hambai	wagon service
トイレ	toire	toilet
女	onna	women
男	otoko	men
和式	washiki	Japanese style
洋式	yooshiki	western style
スーツケース	suutsukeesu	suitcase

On the street (places and related words)

銀行	ginkoo	bank
薬局	yakkyoku	pharmacy
郵便局	yuubinkyoku	post office
旅館	ryokan	Japanese inn
ホテル	hoteru	hotel
ビジネスホテル	bijinesu hoteru	business hotel
レストラン	resutoran	restaurant
喫茶店	kissaten	coffee shop
モーニング サービス	mooningu saabisu	morning service
クリーニング	kuriiningu	dry cleaner's
スーパー	suupaa	supermarket
警察	keisatsu	police station
交番	kooban	police box
宅配	takuhai	home rapid delivery
カラオケ	karaoke	Karaoke
空室	kuushitsu	room available
満室	manshitsu	no room/ no vacancies
開店	kaiten	shop is open
閉店	heiten	shop is closed
緊急	kinkyuu	emergency

On the street (other road signs)

危険	kiken	danger
止まれ	tomare	stop
渡れ	watare	cross
工事中	koojichuu	under construction
禁止	kinshi	prohibited
立ち入り禁止	tachiiri kinshi	no entry
右折	usetsu	right turning
左折	sasetsu	left turning
直進	chokushin	straight on
一方通行	ippoo tsuukoo	one way
歩道	hodoo	pedestrians path
自転車	jitensha	bicycle
自動車	jidoosha	automobile
歩行者	hokoosha	pedestrians
歩道橋	hodookyoo	pedestrian bridge
信号	shingoo	traffic signal

Outside the station/ taxi stands

駐車場	chuushajoo	parking lot
パーキング	paakingu	parking
駐車禁止	chuusha kinshi	no parking
バス	basu	bus
タクシー	takushii	taxi
小型車	kogata-sha	small vehicle
大型車	oogata-sha	large vehicle
空車	kuu-sha	car available

At the restaurant/shop

朝食	chooshoku	breakfast
昼食	chuushoku	lunch
夕食	yuushoku	dinner
和食	washoku	Japanese meals
洋食	yooshoku	western meals
満席	manseki	full (seat)
消費税	shoohizei	Consumer tax
サービス料	saabisu-ryoo	service charge
税サ込み	zeisa-komi	tax and service charge inclusive
税サ別	zeisa-betsu	tax and service charge exclusive
飲み物	nomimono	drinks

English – Japanese

A

a, an		see grammar
abroad	海外	kaigai
accelerator	アクセル	akuseru
to accept	受理します	juri shimasu (dic. juri suru*)
do you accept credit cards?	クレジットカードでもいいですか	kurejitto kaado demo ii desu ka?
accident (traffic, etc.)	事故	jiko
accident and emergency department	救急病棟	kyuukyuu-byootoo
accommodation	宿泊所	shukuhaku-jo
account (bank)	口座	kooza
ache	痛みます	itami masu (dic. itamu*)
my head aches	頭が痛いです	atama ga itai desu
adaptor (electrical)	アダプター	adaputaa
address	住所	juusho
admission fee	入場料	nyuujooryoo
adult	大人	otona
advance:		
in advance	前もって	maemotte
advance payment	先払い	sakibarai
advertisement	宣伝	senden
advise	アドバイスします	adobaisu shimasu (dic. adobaisu suru*)

English	Japanese	
what do you advise?	どうすれば いいですか？	doo sureba ii desu ka?
afford		
I can't afford (to buy) it	買うことが できません	kaukoto ga dekimasen (dic. dekiru*)
afternoon	午後	gogo
in the afternoon	午後に	gogo ni
this afternoon	今日の午後	kyoo no gogo
again	また	mata
age (person's)	年歳	toshi
	時代	jidai
agenda (for meeting)	会議事項	kaigi jikoo
ago	前	mae
a week ago	一週間前	isshuu-kan mae

to agree (support a proposal)	賛成します	sansei shimasu (dic. sansei suru*)
I agree	賛成です	sansei desu
I don't agree	賛成しません	sansei shimasen
aid (charity)	援助	enjo
AIDS	エイズ	eizu
air	空気	kuuki
air conditioning	エアコン	eakon
air pollution	大気汚染	taiki-osen
air hostess	スチュワー デス	suchuwaadesu
airline	航空会社	kookuu-gaisha
airmail	エアメール、 航空便	eameeru, kookuubin
airport	空港	kuukoo
airport bus	空港バス	kuukoo-basu

English – Japanese

English – Japanese

English	Romaji	Japanese	Romaji
alarm (in bank, shop)	keihoo	警報	
alarm clock	mezamashi-dokei	目覚し時計	
alcohol	(o-)sake	(お)酒	
all	zembu	全部	
allergy	arerugii	アレルギー	
I'm allergic to shellfish	kai-rui no arerugii desu	貝類のアレルギーです	
allow	kyoka shimasu (dic. kyoka suru*)	許可します	
is it allowed?	ii desu ka	いいですか	
alone	hitori	一人	
always	itsumo	いつも	
a.m. (before noon)	gozen	午前	
ambulance	kyuukyuu-sha	救急車	

America	Amerika	アメリカ
American (adj)	Amerika-no	アメリカの
(person)	Amerika-jin	アメリカ人
anaesthetic (n)	masui	麻酔
ancestor	senzo	先祖
ancient	kodai-no	古代の
and (furthermore)	soshite (sarani)	そして (さらに)
and	to	と
angina	kyooshin-shoo	狭心症
angry	okotte imasu (dic. okotte iru*)	怒っています
animal	doobutsu	動物
ankle	ashi-kubi	足首
anniversary	kinembi	記念日
wedding anniversary	kekkon kinembi	結婚記念日

another		
(a different kind)	他の	hoka no
I'd like another	他の物が欲しいです	hoka no mono ga hoshii desu
(one more)	もうひとつ	moo hitotsu
answer (written)	返事	henji
(spoken)	答え	kotae
answering machine	留守番電話	rusuban denwa
antibiotic (n)	抗生物質	koosei busshitsu
antihistamine (n)	抗ヒスタミン剤	koo-hisutamin-zai
antiseptic (n)	殺菌剤	sakkin-zai
anyone	誰でも	dare demo
anything	何でも	nan demo
anywhere	どこでも	doko demo
apartment	アパート	apaato

apologies		
my apologies! (formal)	お詫び お詫びいたします	owabi owabi itashimasu
(informal)	ごめんなさい	gomennasai
appendicitis	盲腸炎	moochoo-en
appetite	食欲	shokuyoku
apple juice	りんごジュース	ringo juusu
application (job)	申し込み	mooshikomi
appointment	約束	yakusoku
April	四月	shi-gatsu
are:	あります	arimasu
are there any...?	...がありますか?	...ga arimasu ka? (dic. aru*)
arm	腕	ude

English – Japanese

English	Japanese	
to arrange	手配します	tehai shimasu (dic. tehai suru*)
can we arrange a meeting?	ミーティングを開いてもいいですか	miitingu o hiraitemo ii desu ka?
arrivals (airport)	到着	toochaku
to arrive	到着します	toochaku shimasu (dic. toochaku suru*)
art	芸術	geijutsu
art gallery	美術館	bijutsu-kan
arthritis	関節炎	kansetsu-en
artist	芸術家	geijutsu-ka
as: as soon as possible	出来るだけ早く	dekiru dake hayaku
ashtray	灰皿	haizara
Asia	アジア	Ajia
to ask	聞きます	kiki masu (dic. kiku*)
aspirin	アスピリン	asupirin;
do you have any aspirin?	頭痛薬 頭痛薬はありますか	zutsuu-yaku zutsuu-yaku wa arimasu ka?
assistant (shop)	店員	tenin
asthma	喘息	zensoku
I get asthma	喘息です	zensoku desu
at	で；に	de; ni
at home	家で	uchi de
at 4 o'clock	四時に	yoji ni
atmosphere (of place)	雰囲気	funiki
attractive	魅力的な	minyokuteki-na
audience (theatre etc)	聴衆	chooshuu

English	Japanese	Romaji		English	Japanese	Romaji
August	八月	hachi-gatsu		**avalanche**	雪崩れ	nadare
aunt (own)	おば	oba		**away**	留守	rusu
(somebody else's)	おばさん	oba-san		*I will be away*	八月は留守	hachi-gatsu wa
Australia	オーストラ	oosutoraria		*in August*	です	rusu desu
	リア					
Australian (adj)	オーストラリ	oosutoraria-no		**B**		
	アの			**baby**	赤ちゃん	aka-chan
(person)	オーストラリ	oosutoraria-jin		**baby food**	離乳食	rinyuu-shoku
	ア人			**baby seat**	ベビーシート	bebii shiito
author	著者	chosha		**back** (of body)	背中	senaka
automatic (door)	自動（ドア）	jidoo (doa)		(v) (be back)	戻ります	modorimasu
autumn	秋	aki				(dic. modoru*)
available	入手できます	nyuushu dekimasu		*when will he*	いつ戻りま	itsu modorimasu
		(dic. nyuushu		*be back?*	すか	ka?
		dekiru*)		*I'd like to go*	帰りたいです	kaeritai desu
when will it	いつ頃できま	itsu goro		*back*		
be available?	すか	dekimasu ka?				

English – Japanese

bad (character, morally)	悪い	warui
(food)	腐った	kusatta
bag	鞄	kaban
baggage	荷物	nimotsu
baggage reclaim	手荷物受取所	tenimotsu uketori-sho
baker's	パン屋	pan-ya
ball	ボール	booru
bandage	包帯	hootai
bank	銀行	ginkoo
bar (to drink in)	バー；居酒屋	baa ; izakaya
barber's	床屋	toko-ya
bargain	セール	seeru
baseball	野球	yakyuu
basement	地下	chika
basket	籠	kago
basketball	バスケットボール	basukettobooru
bath	風呂	furo
bathroom	浴室	yokushitsu
bath towel	バスタオル	basu taoru
bath (tub)	浴槽	yokusoo
battery (for radio, etc)	電池	denchi
(for car)	バッテリー	batterii
beach	浜辺	hamabe
bean	豆	mame
bean curd	豆腐	toofu
beautiful	きれい	kirei
bed (western)	ベッド	beddo
(Japanese)	布団	futon
double bed	ダブルベッド	daburu beddo

single bed	シングルベッ ド	shinguru beddo			
bedding	寝具	shingu			
bedroom	寝室	shinshitsu			
beef	牛肉	gyuu-niku			
beer	ビール	biiru			
draught beer	生ビール	nama biiru			
before	前 (に)	mae (ni)			
before 4 o'clock	四時前に	yo-ji mae ni			
before next week	今週中に	konshuu chuu ni			
to begin	始まります	hajimarimasu (dic. hajimaru*)			
to begin	始めます	hajimemasu (dic. hajimeru*)			
(something)					
to belong to	属します	zokushimasu (dic. zokusuru*)			

			it/they	私のです	watashi no desu
			belong(s) to me		
			does this belong to you?	あなたので す か	anata no desu ka?
			belt	ベルト	beruto
			beside	隣	tonari
			can I sit beside you?	隣に座っても いいですか	tonari ni suwatte mo ii desu ka?
			I like this the best	これが一番好 きです	kore ga ichiban suki desu
			best	一番	ichiban
			bicycle	自転車	jitensha
			big	大きい	ookii
			bigger	もっと大きい	motto ookii
			have you anything bigger?	もっと大きい のはありま せんか	motto ookii no wa arimasen ka?

178 | 179

English – Japanese

English	Japanese	Romaji
bike	自転車	jitensha
mountain bike	マウンテンバイク	maunten baiku
bill	(お)勘定	(o-) kanjoo
binoculars	望遠鏡	booenkyoo
bird	鳥	tori
birthday	誕生日	tanjoobi
happy birthday!	誕生日おめでとう!	omedetoo!
birthday present	誕生日プレゼント	tanjoobi purezento
biscuits	ビスケット	bisuketto
bit	少し	sukoshi
just a bit	ほんの少し	hon no sukoshi
to bite	噛みます	kamimasu (dic. kamu*)
bitter (taste)	苦い	nigai

English	Japanese	Romaji
black (n)	黒	kuro
(adj)	黒い；黒の	kuroi; kurono
blanket	毛布	moofu
to bleed	血が出ます	chi ga demasu (dic. chi ga deru*)
it won't stop bleeding	血が止まりません	chi ga tomarimasen
blind (person)	盲目	moomoku
(for window)	ブラインド	buraindo
blocked	詰まった	tsumatta
the sink is blocked	流しが詰まっています	nagashi ga tsumatte imasu
blood	血；血液	chi; ketsueki
blood group	血液型	ketsueki-gata

English	Japanese	Romaji
my blood group is B	(私の)血液型はBです	(watashi no) ketsueki-gata wa 'B' desu
blood pressure	血圧	ketsuatsu
I have high blood pressure	私は高血圧です	watashi wa koo-ketsuatsu desu
blue (n)	青	ao
(adj)	青い	aoi
to board (plane, train)	乗ります	norimasu (dic. noru*)
boarding pass	搭乗券	toojoo-ken
boat	ボート	booto
boiled rice	ご飯	gohan
bone	骨	hone
bonito	鰹	katsuo
book (reading)	本	hon

English	Japanese	Romaji
to book	予約します	yoyaku shimasu (dic. yoyaku suru*)
booking	予約	yoyaku
boots	ブーツ	buutsu
born	生まれます	umaremasu (dic. umareru*)
I was born in Scotland	(私は)スコットランドで生まれました	Skottorando de umaremashita (watashi wa)
to borrow	…を借ります	karimasu (dic. kariru*)
can I borrow...?	…を借りてもいいですか	...o karite mo ii desu ka?
botanical gardens	植物園	shokubutsu-en
bottle	瓶；ボトル	bin; botoru

English – Japanese

English	Japanese	
bottle opener	栓抜き	sennuki
bowl	ボール ; 椀	booru ; wan
box	箱	hako
boy	男の子	otokonoko
boyfriend	彼 ; 彼氏	kare ; kareshi
bra	ブラジャー	burajaa
brakes	ブレーキ	bureeki
branch (bank)	支店	shiten
(company)	社	shisha
(of tree)	枝	eda
brandy	ブランデー	burandee
bread	パン	pan
to break	壊します	kowashimasu (dic. kowasu*)
It has broken down	故障しました	koshoo shimashita

breakfast	朝食 ; 朝ご飯	chooshoku ; asa-gohan
breast (chicken)	(鶏の) 胸肉	(tori-no) mune-niku
to breathe	息をします	iki o shimasu (dic. iki o suru*)
I can't breathe	息ができません	iki ga dekimasen
bride	新婦	shimpu
bridegroom	新郎	shinroo
bridge (game)	ブリッジ	burijji
bridge (over river, road, etc.)	橋	hashi
briefcase	ブリーフケース	buriifu keesu

English	Japanese	Romaji
to bring (thing)	持って来ます	motte kimasu (dic. motte kuru*)
(person)	連れて来ます	tsurete kimasu (dic. tsurete kuru*)
Britain	イギリス；英国	Igirisu ; Eikoku
British (adj)	英国の	Eikoku-no
(person)	英国人	Eikoku-jin
brochure	パンフレット	panfuretto
brothers	兄弟	kyoodai
brother (own, younger)	弟	otooto
(own, older)	兄	ani
(somebody else's, younger)	弟さん	otooto-san
(somebody else's, older)	お兄さん	onii-san
brown (n)	茶色	chairo
(adj)	茶色い	chairoi
Buddha	仏	hotoke
Buddhism	仏教	bukkyoo
Buddhist temple	(お)寺	(o-) tera
building	建物；ビル	tatemono ; biru
bulb (light)	電球	denkyuu
bullet train	新幹線	Shinkansen
bureau de change	両替所	ryoogae-jo
burn	こがします	kogashimasu (dic. kogasu*)
It's burnt (food)	こげています	kogete imasu
bus	バス	basu
by bus	バスで	merishi

English – Japanese

business	ビジネス；仕事	bijinesu ; shigoto
business card	名刺	merishi
business trip	出張	shucchoo
bus stop	バス停	basutei
bus tour	バスツアー	basu tsuaa
is there a bus tour?	バスツアーがありますか	basu tsuaa ga arimasu ka?
busy	忙しい	isogashii
are you busy?	忙しいですか	isogashii desu ka?
the line is busy (phone)	話中です	hanashi-chuu desu
butcher's	肉屋	nikuya
butter	バター	bataa
button	ボタン	botan

to buy	買います	kaimasu
		(dic. kau*)
where can I buy...?	どこで買えますか	doko de kaemasu ka?

C

cable car	ケーブルカー	keeburukaa
caddy (golf)	キャディー	kyadii
café	喫茶店	kissaten
cake (western style)	ケーキ	keeki
cake shop	ケーキ屋	keeki-ya
calculator	計算機	keisanki
to call (phone)	...に電話をかけます	...ni denwa o kakemasu (dic. denwa o kakeru*)

English	Japanese	Romaji
long-distance call	長距離電話	chookyori denwa
camcorder	ビデオカメラ	bideo kamera
camera	カメラ	kamera
camera shop	カメラ屋	kamera-ya
camping	キャンプ	kyampu
can (n)	缶	kan
can (v)	出来ます	dekimasu (dic. dekiru*)
can I...?	...出来ますか	...dekimasu ka?
Canada	カナダ	Kanada
Canadian (adj)	カナダの	Kanada-no
(person)	カナダ人	Kanada-jin
to cancel	取り消します	torikeshimasu (dic. torikesu*)

English	Japanese	Romaji
I'd like to cancel my booking	予約を取り消したいです	yoyaku o torikeshitai desu
cancellation		kekkoo
(of flight)	欠航	unkyuu
(of train)	運休	
cancer	癌	gan
canned	缶詰	kanzume
can opener	缶切	kankiri
capital (city)	首都	shuto
(money)	資金	shikin
car	車；自動車	kuruma; jidoosha
caravan	キャラバン	kyaraban
card (business)	名刺	merishi
(playing)	トランプ	torampu
(greetings)	カード	kaado
cardphone	カード用電話	kaado-yoo denwa

English – Japanese

English – Japanese

careful	気をつけます	ki o tsukemasu (dic. ki o tsukeru*)	
be careful!	気をつけて!	ki o tsukete!	
careless	不注意	fuchuui	
car keys	車の鍵	kuruma no kagi	
car park	駐車場	chuushajoo	
carpet	絨毯 ; カーペット	juutan ; kaapetto	
carriage (train)	客車	kyakusha	
carrier bag	買い物袋	kaimono bukuro	
carrot	人参	ninjin	
to carry	運びます	hakobimasu (dic. hakobu*)	
carsick	車酔い	kurumayoi	

I get carsick	車に酔います	kuruma ni yoimasu (dic. kuruma ni you*)	
carwash	洗車	sensha	
case (suitcase)	スーツケース ; 旅行鞄	suutsukeesu ; ryokoukaban	
cash (n)	現金	genkin	
we only take cash	現金払いのみです	genkin barai nomi desu	
casino	カジノ	kajino	
castle	城	shiro	
cat	猫	neko	
to catch (hold of)	掴みます	tsukamimasu (dic. tsukamu*)	
to catch a cold	風邪をひきます	kaze o hikimasu (dic. kaze o hiku*)	

English	Japanese		English	Japanese	
cathedral	大聖堂	daiseidoo	century	世紀	seiki
Catholic	カトリック教	katorikku-kyoo	21st century	二十一世紀	niju̅u-isseiki
cauliflower	カリフラワー	karifurawaa	ceramics	陶器	tooki
cave	洞窟	dookutsu	certain	確か	tashika
CD	シーディー	shiidii	are you certain?	本当ですか	hontoo desu ka?
CD player	シーディープレーヤー	shiidii pureiyaa	certainly! (truth)	確かに	tashika-ni
			certainly!	喜んで!	yorokonde!
cell phone	携帯電話	keitai denwa	(I will do that)		
cemetery	墓地	bochi	chair	椅子	isu
centigrade	摂氏	sesshi	champagne	シャンペン	shampen
centimetre	センチ（メートル）	senchi (meetoru)	change (money)	小銭	kozeni
			changing room	更衣室	kooi-shitsu
central	中心の	chuushin-no	charge (fee)	手数料	tesuuryoo
central heating	セントラルヒーティング	sentoraru hiitingu	is there any charge?	手数料はかかりますか	tesuuryoo wa kakarimasu ka?
centre	中心；中央	chuushin ; chuuoo	free of charge	無料	muryoo

to check	調べます ； チェックします	shirabemasu (dic. shiraberu*) ； chekku shimasu (dic. chekku suru*)	to check out	チェックアウトします	chekku-auto shimasu (dic. chekku-auto suru*)
can you check this for me?	これを調べてください	kore o shirabete kudasai	When should I check out by?	チェックアウトは何時ですか	chekku-auto wa nan-ji desu ka?
to check in	チェックインします	chekku-in shimasu (dic. chekku-in suru*)	cheese	チーズ	chiizu
			chef	シェフ	shefu
where do I check in?	チェックインはどこでしますか	chekku-in wa dokode shimasuka?	chemist's (shop)	薬屋 ； 薬局	kusuriya ； yakkyoku
			cheque	チェック ； 小切手	chekku ； kogitte
check-in desk (hotel)	フロント	furonto	cherry blossom	桜	sakura
			chest (of body)	胸	mune
			chewing gum	チューインガム	chuuin-gamu

chicken (bird)	鶏	niwatori
(meat)	鶏肉	toriniku
(grilled)	焼き鳥	yaki-tori
chickenpox	水痘瘡	mizuboosoo
children	子供達	kodomotachi
chilli	唐辛子	toogarashi
china (n)	瀬戸物	setomono
China	中国	Chuugoku
Chinese (adj)	中国の	Chuugoku-no
(person)	中国人	Chuugoku-jin
(language)	中国語	Chuugoku-go
chips (french fries)	フライドポテト	furaido poteto
chocolate(s)	チョコレート	chokoreeto
to choose	選びます	erabimasu
		(dic. erabu*)

I don't know	どれにしたら	dore ni shitara ii
what to choose	いいかわか	ka wakarimasen
	りません	
you choose	代わりに選ん	kawari ni erande
for me	でください	kudasai
chopsticks	(お)箸	(o-)hashi
Christmas	クリスマス	kurisumasu
Christmas Eve	クリスマス	kurisumasu-ibu
	イブ	
church	教会	kyookai
cigar	葉巻	hamaki
cigarette	煙草	tabako
cigarette	ライター	raitaa
lighter		
cinema	映画館	eiga-kan
city	町；都会	machi；tokai

English – Japanese

English – Japanese

English	Japanese	romaji
city centre	町の中心	machi no chuushin
claim (n)	要求	yookyuu
class (in school)	組；クラス	kumi; kurasu
business class	ビジネスクラス	bijinesu kurasu
economy class	エコノミークラス	ekonomii kurasu
first class	ファーストクラス	faasuto kurasu
classical music	音楽	ongaku
clean (adj)	きれいな	kirei-na
to clean (house)	掃除します	sooji shimasu (dic. sooji suru*)
cleaner (company)	清掃業者	seisoo gyoosha

English	Japanese	romaji
clever	賢い	kashikoi
climate	気候；風土	kikoo; fuudo
climbing (mountains)	山登り	yama nobori
climbing boots	登山靴	tozan gutsu
clinic	クリニック；診療所	kurinikku; shinryoo-jo
clock	時計	tokei
to close	閉めます	shimemasu (dic. shimeru*)
when do you close?	いつ閉まりますか	itsu shimarimasu ka?
closed (shops)	閉店	heiten
clothes	服	fuku
cloudy	曇っている	kumotte-iru
club	クラブ	kurabu
clutch (car)	クラッチ	kuratchi

English	Japanese	
coach (bus)	バス	basu
(of train)	客車	kyakusha
coach station	バス乗り場	basu noriba
coast	海岸	kaigan
coat	コート；上着	kooto ; uwagi
Coca Cola®	コカコーラ	kokakoora
coffee	コーヒー	koohii
black coffee	ブラックコーヒー	burakku koohii
white coffee	ミルクコーヒー	miruku koohii
decaffeinated coffee	カフェイン抜きのコーヒー	kafein nuki no koohii
cappuccino	カプチーノ	kapuchiino
cognac	コニャック	konyakku
coin	コイン；…玉	koin ; -dama
ten-yen coin	十円玉	ju-en-dama
cold (room)	寒い	samui
I have a cold	風邪をひいています	kaze o hiite imasu
colleague	同僚	dooryoo
college (university)	大学	daigaku
(junior college)	短大	tandai
colour	色	iro
colour film (for camera)	カラーフィルム	karaa firumu
comb	櫛	kushi
to come	来ます	kimasu (dic. kuru*)
when can you come?	いつ来られますか	itsu koraremasuka
come in!	どうぞお入りください	doozo ohairi kudasai

English – Japanese

English	Japanese	Romaji
comedy	コメディー	komedii
comfortable	気持ちがいい	kimochi ga ii
this is very comfortable	これはとても気持ちがいいです	kore wa totemo kimochi ga ii desu
comics (publications)	漫画	manga
commercial (on TV)	コマーシャル	komaasharu
common (usual)	普通の	futsuu-no
compact disc	コンパクトディスク；シーディー	kompakuto disuku ; shii dii
company (firm)	会社	kaisha
company president	社長；常務	shachoo ; joomu
compartment (train)	車両	sharyoo
complaint	苦情	kujoo
I have a complaint	苦情があります	kujoo ga arimasu
to complete	完成します	kansei shimasu (dic. kansei suru*)
complicated	複雑な	fukuzatsu na
it's very complicated	とても複雑です	totemo fukuzatsu desu
compulsory	義務	gimu
computer	コンピューター	kompyuutaa
computer game	コンピューターゲーム	kompyuutaa geemu
concert	コンサート	konsaato

English	Japanese	
concert hall	コンサート ホール	konsaato hooru
concussion (brain)	脳震盪	nooshintoo
conditioner (hair)	リンス	rinsu
condom	コンドーム	kondoomu
conductor (music)	指揮者	shikisha
conference	会議	kaigi
conference centre	会議場	kaigijoo
to confirm	確認します	kakunin shimasu (dic. kakunin suru*)

	Japanese	
do I need to confirm?	確認する必要 がありますか	kakunin suru hitsuyoo ga arimasu ka
I want to confirm my booking	予約の確認を お願いします	yoyaku no kakunin o onegai shimasu
congratulations	おめでとう ございます	omedetoo gozaimasu
to connect	つなぎます	tsunagimasu (dic. tsunagu*)
I'm trying to connect you	おつなぎして います	otsunagi shite imasu
connection (train, plane)	乗り継ぎ	noritsugi
(electronic)	接続	setsuzoku
constipated	便秘	benpi
I'm constipated	便秘です	benpi desu

English – Japanese

consul	領事	ryooji
consulate	領事館	ryoojikan
contact lens	コンタクトレンズクリーナー	kontakuto renzu
cleaner		kuriinaa
contact lenses	コンタクトレンズ	kontakuto renzu
continent	大陸	tairiku
contraceptive (n)	避妊薬；避妊用品	hinin-yaku; hinin-yoohin
convenient	便利な；都合のいい	benri-na; tsugoo no ii
cook (n) (Japanese restaurants)	コック 板前	kokku itamae
to cook	料理します	ryoori shimasu (dic. ryoori suru*)

copy (n)	コピー	kopii
can I make a copy?	コピーをしてもいいですか	kopii o shitemo ii desu ka
corkscrew	栓抜き	sen-nuki
corn	とうもろこし	toomorokoshi
corner	角	kado
correct	正しい	tadashii
is it correct?	正しいですか	tadashii desu ka
corridor	廊下	rooka
cost (n)	費用；コスト	hiyoo ; kosuto
to cost	かかります	kakarimasu (dic. kakaru*)
how much does it cost?	いくらかかりますか	ikura kakarimasu ka
cotton	綿	wata/men
cough (n)	咳	seki

to count	数えます	kazoemasu (dic. kazoeru*)
country	国	kuni
countryside	田舎	inaka
courier	宅配	takuhai
course	コース	koosu
of course	勿論	mochiron
court (law)	法廷	hootei
(tennis)	テニスコート	tenisu kooto
crab	蟹	kani
crafts	工芸品	koogei hin
cramp	痙攣;こむらがえり	keiren; komuragaeri
crayfish	ザリガニ	zarigani
cream	クリーム	kuriimu
credit	信用	shinyoo
credit card	クレジットカード	kurejitto kaado
crisps	ポテトチップス	poteto chippusu
crossing (ferry)	フェリー	ferii
when is the next crossing?	次のフェリーは何時ですか	tsugi no ferii wa nanji desu ka
crossroads	十字路	juujiro
crowd	人ごみ	hitogomi
cruise (n)	船旅	funatabi
to cry (weep)	泣きます	nakimasu (dic. naku*)
cup	カップ	kappu
cupboard	戸棚	todana

English – Japanese

English - Japanese

English	Japanese	romaji
to cure	治療します	chiryoo shimasu (dic. chiryoo suru*)
current (electricity)	電流	denryuu
curtains	カーテン	kaaten
cushion	クッション	kusshion
customs	税関	zeikan
customs declaration	税関申告	zeikan shinkoku
cut (n)	切り傷	kirikizu
to cut	切ります	kirimasu (dic. kiru*)
cybercafé	インターネットカフェ	intaanetto kafe
cycling	サイクリング	saikuringu

D

daily (each day)	毎日の	mainichi-no
dance	踊り；ダンス	odori; dansu
to dance	踊ります	odorimasu (*dic. odoru)
dangerous	危ない；危険	abunai; kiken
dark	暗い	kurai
date (day of month)	日付	hizuke
date of birth	生年月日	seinen-gappi
daughter (own)	娘	musume
daughter (somebody else's)	娘さん；お嬢さん	musume-san; o-joo-san
day	日	nichi
per day	一日に	ichi-nichi ni
every day	毎日	mai-nichi

English	Japanese	
deaf	耳の聞こえない	mimi no kikoenai
dear (expensive)	高い；高価い	takai; kooka i
decaffeinated	カフェイン抜きの	kafein nuki-no
December	十二月	juuni-gatsu
deep	深い	fukai
degree (temperature)	度	do
degree (university)	学位	gakui
delay	遅れ	okure
how long is the delay?	どのぐらい遅れますか	donogurai okuremasuka
to be delayed (plane, train, etc)	遅れます	okuremasu (dic. okureru*)
dentist	歯医者	ha-isha
dentures	義歯；入れ歯	gishi; ireba
department store	デパート	depaato
departure	出発	shuppatsu
departure lounge	出発ラウンジ	shuppatsu raunji
deposit (to pay)	保証金	hoshookin
dessert	デザート	dezaato
destination	目的地	mokutekichi
detergent	洗剤	senzai
diabetes	糖尿病	toonyoobyoo
to dial	ダイヤルします	daiyaru shimasu (dic. daiyaru suru*)
dialling code	局番	kyokuban
diarrhoea	下痢	geri
diary	日記	nikki
dictionary	辞書	jisho

English – Japanese

English – Japanese

different	違う	chigau
digital camera	デジタルカメラ	dejitaru kamera
dining room	ダイニングルーム；食堂	daininguruumu; shokudoo
dinner	夕食；ディナー	yuushoku; dinaa
direct (train, etc.)	直通	chokutsuu
direction	方向	hookoo
directory (telephone)	電話帳	denwa-choo
dirty	汚い	kitanai
disabled	障害のある	shoogai no aru
disco	ディスコ	disuko
discount	割引	waribiki
dish	（お）皿	(o-)sara
disinfectant	消毒薬	shoodoku-yaku
disk	ディスク	disuku
disposable	使い捨ての	tsukaisute-no
district	地方	chihoo
divorce (n)	離婚	rikon
divorced	離婚した	rikonshita
dizzy	眩暈	memai
to feel dizzy	眩暈がします	memai ga shimasu (dic. memai ga suru*)
to do	します	shimasu (dic. suru*)
doctor	医者	isha
document	文書	bunsho
dog	犬	inu
dollar	ドル	doru
door	戸；ドア	to; doa

English	Japanese	Romaji
double (quantity)	二重の	nijuu-no
	二倍の	nibai-no
double bed	ダブルベッド	daburu beddo
double room	ダブルルーム；二人部屋	daburu ruumu; futari beya
download	ダウンロードします	daunroodo shimasu (dic. daunroodo suru*)
dress (n)	ドレス	doresu
dressing (medical)	包帯	hootai
dressing (salad)	ドレッシング	doresshingu
drink	飲み物	nomimono
to drink	飲みます	nomimasu (dic. nomu*)
to drive	運転します；ドライブします	unten shimasu (dic. unten suru); doraibu shimasu (dic. doraibu suru*)
driver (of car)	運転手	untenshu
driving licence	運転免許証	unten-menkyoshoo
drug (medical)	薬；薬品	kusuri; yakuhin
to dry (clothes, etc)	乾かします	kawakashimasu (dic. kawakasu*)
dry-cleaner's	ドライクリーニング	dorai-kuriiningu
duck	アヒル	ahiru
duty-free	免税の	menzei-no
duvet	掛け布団	kakebuton

English – Japanese

English – Japanese

E

ear	耳	mimi	
earache	耳が痛い	mimi ga itai	
early	早く	hayaku	
earplugs	耳栓	mimi-sen	
earrings	イヤリング	iyaringu	
earthquake	地震	jishin	
east	東	higashi	
Easter	イースター	iisutaa	
to eat	食べます	tabemasu	
		(dic. taberu*)	
eel	うなぎ	unagi	
egg	卵；玉子	tamago	
fried egg	目玉焼き	medama-yaki	
hard-boiled egg	硬ゆで卵	kata yude tamago	
scrambled eggs	炒り玉子	iri tamago	
elastic	輪ゴム	wa-gomu	

electrician	電気屋	denkiya	
electricity	電気；電力	denki; denryoku	
electric razor	電気かみそり	denki-kamisori	
elevator	エレベーター	erebeetaa	
e-mail	電子メール；イーメール	denshi-meeru; ii-meeru	
embassy	大使館	taishikan	
emergency	緊急	kinkyuu	
emergency exit	非常口	hijoo-guchi	
emperor	天皇	tennoo	
empty	空	kara	
engaged (couple)	婚約している	konyaku shite-iru	
(phone)	話し中	hanashi-chuu	
(toilet)	使用中	shiyoo-chuu	
England	イギリス	Igirisu	

English (adj)	イギリスの	Igirisu-no
(person)	イギリス人	Igirisu-jin
(language)	英語	Eigo
enough	十分	juubun
that's enough	もう結構です	moo kekkoo desu
(food, etc.)		
enquiry desk	受付	uketsuke
to enter (a place)	入ります	hairimasu
		(dic. hairu*)
entrance	入口	iriguchi
entrance fee	入場料	nyuu-joo-ryoo
envelope	封筒	futoo
equipment	設備	setsubi
escalator	エスカレー	esukareetaa
	ター	
euro	ユーロ	yuuro
Europe	ヨーロッパ	yooroppa

evening	夜；晩	yoru ; ban
in the evening	夜に	yoru ni
evening meal	夕食；夕飯	yuushoku ; yuuhan
example	例	rei
for example	たとえば	tatoeba
excellent	素晴らしい	subarashii
excess baggage	超過手荷物	chooka tenimotsu
exchange rate	為替レート	kawase reeto
excursion	遠足	ensoku
excuse me	すみません	sumimasen
exhibition	展示会	tenjikai
exit	出口	deguchi
expensive	高価な	kooka-na
exports	輸出品	yushutsu-hin
express train	急行	kyuukoo

English – Japanese

English – Japanese

extension (electrical)	延長コード	enchoo koodo	Far East	極東	kyokutoo
(phone)	内線	naisen	farm	農家	nooka
eye	目	me	fast	速い	hayai
eye drops	目薬	megusuri	fat (person)	太った	futotta
			father (own)	父	chichi
F			(somebody else's)	お父さん	otoo-san
fabric	生地	kiji	faulty (machine, etc.)	欠陥のある	kekkan no aru
factory	工場	koojoo	fax	ファックス	fakkusu
to faint	気絶します (dic. kizetsu suru)	kizetsu shimasu	fax number	ファックス番号	fakkusu bangoo
false teeth	入れ歯	ireba	to fax	ファックスを送ります	fakkusu o okurimasu (dic. fakkusu o okuru*)
family	家族	kazoku			
fan (hand-held)	うちわ；扇子	uchiwa ; sensu	February	二月	ni-gatsu
(electric)	扇風機	senpuu-ki	fee	料金	ryookin
far	遠い	tooi			
fare (bus, etc.)	料金	ryookin			

female (adj)	女の	onna-no
ferry	フェリー	ferii
festival	祭り	matsuri
a few	いくつかの	ikutsuka-no
few	二、三の	ni, san no
fiancé(e)	フィアンセ ; 婚約者	fianse ; konyaku-sha
file (computer, document)	ファイル	fairu
filling (tooth)	詰め物	tsumemono
film (for camera)	フィルム	firumu
film (cinema)	映画	eiga
to find	見つけます	mitsukemasu (dic. mitsukeru*)
I can't find...	…が見つかりません	...ga mitsukari masen
fine (penalty)	罰金	bakkin

finger	指	yubi
fire	火	hi
house fire	家事 ; 火災	kaji ; kasai
camp fire	焚き火	takibi
fire alarm	火災報知器	kasai-hoochi-ki
fire brigade	消防隊	shooboo-tai
fire escape	非常階段	hijoo-kaidan
fire extinguisher	消火器	shookaki
fireworks	花火	hanabi
firm (company)	会社	kaisha
first	最初の	saisho-no
first aid	応急手当	ookyuu-teate
first aid kit	救急箱	kyuukyuu-bako
first class	ファーストクラス	faasuto kurasu
first floor (above ground floor)	二階	ni-kai

English – Japanese

English – Japanese

first name	名前	namae
fish (n)	魚	sakana
to fit	合います	aimasu (dic. au*)
it doesn't fit	合いません	aimasen
fitting room	試着室	shichaku-shitsu
to fix	直します	naoshimasu (dic. naosu*)
can you fix it?	直せますか	naosemasu ka?
flat (apartment)	アパート	apaato
(battery)	バッテリーが	batterii ga
	あがります	agarimasu (dic. batterii ga agaru*)
flat tyre	パンク	panku
flavour	味	aji
floor (of building)	…階	…kai
first floor	一階	ikkai
second floor	二階	ni-kai
(of room)	床	yuka
flower	花	hana
flu	インフルエンザ	infuruenza
fly (insect)	ハエ	hae
to fly	飛びます	tobimasu (dic. tobu*)
food	食べ物	tabemono
food poisoning	食中毒	shokuchuu-doku
foot	足	ashi
football (soccer)	サッカー	sakkaa
for (in exchange for)	…の代わりに	…no kawari ni
foreign	外国の	gaikoku-no
forest	森	mori
fork (cutlery)	フォーク	fooku

English	Japanese	
fortnight	二週間	ni-shuu-kan
fountain	泉; 噴水	izumi; funsui
foyer	ロビー	robii
fracture (of bone)	骨折	kossetsu
fragrance	香り	kaori
frame (picture)	額	gaku
free (not occupied)	空いています	aite imasu (dic. aite iru*)
(costing nothing)	無料の	muryoo-no
(not constrained)	自由 (な)	jiyuu (na)
fresh (food)	新鮮 (な)	shinsen (na)
Friday	金曜日	kin-yoobi
fridge	冷蔵庫	reizooko
fried food	揚げ物	agemono
friend	友だち	tomodachi
fruit	果物	kudamono
fruit juice	フルーツジュース	furuutsujuusu
fuel	燃料	nenryoo
full	いっぱい	ippai
full board	三食付の宿泊	san-shoku tsuki no shukuhaku
funny (amusing)	面白い	omoshiroi
(strange)	おかしい; かわった	okashii; kawatta
fuse	ヒューズ	hyuuzu
fuse box	ヒューズボックス	hyuuzu bokkusu

G

gallery	ギャラリー; 画廊	gyararii; garoo
game	ゲーム	geemu

English – Japanese

garage	ガレージ；車庫	gareeji ; shako
garden	庭	niwa
garlic	にんにく	ninniku
gastritis	胃炎	ien
gate	門	mon
(airport)	ゲート；搭乗口	geeto ; toojoo guchi
gay (bright)	華やかな	hanayaka-na
(homosexual)	ゲイ	gei
gears (cogs)	ギア	gia
	歯車	haguruma
generous	寛大な	kandai-na
gentleman	紳士	shinshi
gents (toilet)	男性用トイレ	dansei-yoo toire

to get (obtain)	手に入れます	te ni iremasu (dic. te ni ireru*)
(to fetch something)	持ってきます	motte kimasu (dic. motte kuru*)
(to fetch person, animal)	連れてきます	tsurete kimasu (dic. tsurete kuru*)
to get in (car)	乗ります	norimasu (dic. noru*)
to get off (bus, etc.)	降ります	orimasu (dic. oriru*)
gift	贈り物；プレゼント	okurimono ; purezento
gift shop	ギフトショップ	gifuto shoppu
ginger	しょうが	shooga

girl (informal)	少女；女の子	shoojo; onnanoko	to go in	入ります	hairimasu (dic. hairu*)
(polite)	お嬢さん	ojoo-san	gold	金	kin
girlfriend	彼女	kanojo	golf	ゴルフ	gorufu
to give	あげます	agemasu (dic. ageru*)	golf ball	ゴルフボール	gorufu booru
			golf club	ゴルフクラブ	gorufu kurabu
to give back	返します	kaeshimasu (dic. kaesu*)	golf course	ゴルフコース	gorufu koosu
glass	グラス；コップ	gurasu ; koppu	good	よい；いい	yoi ; ii
			good afternoon	こんにちは	konnichiwa
glasses (spectacles)	めがね	megane	goodbye	さようなら	sayoonara
			good evening	こんばんは	kombanwa
gloves	手袋	tebukuro	good morning	おはようございます	ohayoo gozaimasu
glue	のり	nori	good night	おやすみなさい	oyasuminasai
to go	行きます	ikimasu (dic. iku*)	to go out	出かけます	dekakemasu (dic. dekakeru*)
to go back	戻ります	modorimasu (dic. modoru*)			

English – Japanese

English - Japanese

granddaughter	孫娘	mago-musume	grey (n)	灰色；グレー	haiiro ; guree
grandfather (own)	祖父	sofu	(adj)	灰色の； グレーの	haiiro-no ; guree-no
(somebody else's)	おじいさん	ojii-san	grilled	焼いた； 焼き...	yaita ; yaki...
grandmother (own)	祖母	sobo	grocer's	食料品店	shokuryoohin-ten
(somebody else's)	おばあさん	obaa-san	ground floor	一階	ikkai
grandson	孫息子	mago-musuko	group (people)	グループ；組	guruupu ; kumi
grapefruit	グレープフルーツ	gureepu furuutsu	guarantee (n)	保証	hoshoo
grapes	ぶどう	budoo	guest (to house)	お客様	okyaku-sama
great (large)	大きい	ookii	guest house	ゲストハウス	gesuto hausu
green (n)	緑	midori	guide (n)	ガイド；案内	gaido ; annai
(adj)	緑の	midori-no	to guide	案内をします	annai o shimasu (dic. annai o suru*)
greengrocer	八百屋	yao-ya	guidebook	ガイドブック	gaido bukku
			guided tour	ガイドツアー	gaido tsuaa

H

hair	髪；髪の毛	kami; kaminoke
hairbrush	ブラシ	burashi
haircut	散髪；ヘアーカット	sampatsu; heaakatto
hairdresser's (for men)	床屋	tokoya
(for women)	美容院	biyooin
hair dryer	ヘアードライヤー	heaa doraiyaa
half-price	半額	hangaku
hall (for concerts, etc.)	ホール；館	hooru; kan
ham	ハム	hamu
handbag	ハンドバッグ	handobaggu
handicapped (person)	身体障害者	shintai shoogaisha

handkerchief	ハンカチ	hankachi
hand luggage	手荷物	tenimotsu
hand-made	手作りの	tezukuri-no
to happen	起こります	okorimasu (dic. okoru*)
what happened?	どうしましたか	doo shimashita ka
hard (firm)	かたい	katai
(difficult)	難しい	muzukashii
hay fever	花粉症	kafunshoo
head	頭	atama
headache	頭痛	zutsuu
headlights	ヘッドライト	heddoraito
head office	本社	honsha
headphones	ヘッドホン	heddohon
hearing aid	補聴器	hochooki

English – Japanese

English – Japanese

heart (emotional)	心	kokoro
heart (organ)	心臓	shinzoo
heart attack	心臓発作	shinzoo hossa
to heat up	温めます	atatamemasu
		(dic. atatameru*)
heater	ヒーター	hiitaa
heavy (weight)	重い	omoi
hello	こんにちは	konnichiwa
(on phone)	もしもし	moshi moshi
to help	手伝います	tetsudaimasu
		(dic. tetsudau*)
help!	助けて!	tasukete!
here	ここ	koko
high	高い	takai
high blood pressure	高血圧	koo-ketsuatsu
hill-walking	ハイキング	haikingu

to hire	借ります	karimasu
		(dic. kariru*)
can I hire...?	...を借りられ	...o kariraremasu
	ますか	ka
hobby	趣味	shumi
holiday	休暇 ;	kyuuka ; horidee
	ホリデー	
on holiday	休暇中	kyuuka-chuu
national holiday	祭日	saijitsu
homesick	ホームシック	hoomushikku
honey	はちみつ	hachimitsu
honeymoon	ハネムーン ;	hanemuun ;
	新婚旅行	shinkon ryoko
horse	馬	uma
horseradish (Japanese)	わさび	wasabi

hospital	病院	byooin
hostel	ユースホステル	yuusu hosuteru
hot	あつい	atsui
hotel	ホテル	hoteru
Japanese hotel (traditional) (B&B)	旅館	ryokan
	民宿	minshuku
hour	時間	jikan
one hour	一時間	ichi-jikan
two hours	二時間	ni-jikan
house	家	ie
housewife	主婦	shufu
house wine	ハウスワイン	hausu wain
how	どのぐらい; どうやって	donogurai; dooyatte

how much/ many?	どのぐらい?	dono gurai?
how shall we get there?	どうやって行きましょうか	dooyatte ikimashoo ka
hungry	おなかがすき ます	onaka ga sukimasu (dic. onaka ga suku*)
I'm hungry	おなかがすい ています	onaka ga suite imasu
hurry	急ぎます	isogimasu (dic. isogu*)
I'm in a hurry	急いでいます	isoide imasu
to hurt	痛みます	itamimasu (dic. itamu*)
my back hurts	背中が痛いで す	senaka ga itai desu

English – Japanese

English	Japanese	Romaji
husband (own)	主人	shujin
(somebody else's)	ご主人	go-shujin
I		
I (informal)	わたし	watashi
(polite)	わたくし	watakushi
ice	氷；アイス	koori ; aisu
ice cream	アイスクリーム	aisu kurimu
identity card	身分証明書	mibun shoomei-sho
ill	病気	byooki
...is ill	...は病気です	...wa byooki desu
illegal	違法	ihoo
immediately	すぐに	sugu-ni
important	大切（な）	taisetsu (na)
imports	輸入	yunyuu
indigestion	消化不良	shooka furyoo
inflammation	炎症	enshoo
information	情報	joohoo
information office	案内所	annai-sho
injection	注射	chuusha
to be injured	怪我をします	kega o shimasu (dic. kega o suru*)
insect	昆虫	konchuu
insect repellent	虫除け	mushi-yoke
inside...	...の中に	...no naka ni
inside the car	車の中に	kuruma no naka ni
instant coffee	インスタントコーヒー	insutanto koohii

English	Japanese	Romaji
instructions (for use)	取扱説明書	toriatsukai setsumei sho`
insulin	インシュリン	inshurin
insurance	保険	hoken
insurance certificate	保険証	hokenshoo
international	国際的 (な)	kokusaiteki (na)
Internet	インターネット	intaanetto
Internet café	インターネットカフェ	intaanetto kafe
interpreter (theatre)	通訳	tsuuyaku
interval (theatre)	休憩	kyuukei
to introduce (a person)	紹介します	shookai shimasu (dic. shookai suru*)
invitation	招待	shootai
to invite	招待します	shootai shimasu (dic. shootai suru*)
invoice	請求書	seikyuu-sho
Ireland	アイルランド	Airurando
Irish (adj)	アイルランドの	Airurando-no
(person)	アイルランド人	Airurando-jin
iron (for clothes)	アイロン	airon
(metal)	鉄	tetsu
ironmonger's	金物屋	kanamono-ya
island	島	shima
itemized bill	請求明細書	seikyuu meisaisho

J

jacket	ジャケット	jakketto
jam (food)	ジャム	jamu
traffic jam	交通渋滞	kootsuu juutai
January	一月	ichi-gatsu
Japan	日本	Nihon ; Nippon
Japanese (language)	日本語	Nihon-go
(adj)	日本の	Nihon-no
(person)	日本人	Nihon-jin
jeweller's	宝石店	hooseki-ten
jewellery	宝石	hooseki
job	仕事	shigoto
to jog	ジョギングを します	jogingu o shimasu (dic. jogingu o suru*)
journey	旅行	ryokoo

juice (fruit)	ジュース	juusu
(of something)	汁 ; 液	shiru ; eki
July	七月	shichi-gatsu
junction (roads)	交差点	koosaten
June	六月	roku-gatsu
just...	…だけ ; …ばかり	...dake ; bakari
just two	二つだけ	futatsu dake
I've just arrived	ついたばかり です	tsuita bakari desu

K

key (for lock)	鍵	kagi
kidneys (food)	インゲン豆	ingen mame
kilo	キロ	kiro
kilometre	キロメーター	kiromeetaa

kind (n)	種類	shurui
(adj)	親切 (な)	shinsetsu (na)
kitchen	台所	daidokoro
knickers	パンツ	pantsu
knife	ナイフ	naifu
(Japanese)	包丁	hoochoo
knot	結び目 ; こぶ	musubi-me ; kobu
to know (facts)	知ります	shirimasu
		(dic. shiru*)
I don't know	私は東京を知	watashi wa
	りません	Tookyoo o
		shirimasen
Tokyo		
Korea	韓国	Kankoku

L

label	ラベル	raberu
lace	レース	reesu
shoe lace	靴紐	kutsu-himo
ladies (toilet)	婦人用トイレ	fujin-yoo toire
lake	湖	mizuumi
land (n)	土地	tochi
language	言語 ; 言葉	gengo ; kotoba
large	大きい	ookii
late	遅い	osoi
the train is late	電車が遅れ	densha ga
	ています	okurete imasu
launderette	コインランド	koin randorii
	リー	
laundry service	クリーニング	kuriiningu
lavatory	洗面所	senmenjo
lawyer	弁護士	bengoshi

English – Japanese

English – Japanese

leader (of group)	リーダー	riidaa
leaflet	チラシ	chirashi
leak (n) (of gas, liquid)	漏れ	more
to learn	学びます	manabimasu (dic. manabu*)
leather	革	kawa
to leave	出発します	shuppatsu shimasu (dic. shuppatsu suru) ; 去ります sarimasu (dic. saru*)
(leave behind)	おいていきます	oite ikimasu (dic. oite iku*)
left	左	hidari
on/to the left	左に	hidari ni

left luggage (office)	手荷物一時預 かり所	tenimotsu ichiji azukari-sho
leg	足	ashi
lens	レンズ	renzu
letter (mail)	手紙	tegami
letterbox	郵便受け	yuubin-uke
lettuce	レタス	retasu
library	図書館	toshokan
licence	免許証	menkyoshoo
to lie down	横になります	yoko ni narimasu (dic. yoko ni naru*)
life belt	救命ベルト	kyuumei-beruto
lifeboat	救命ボート	kyuumei-booto
lifeguard	ライフガー ド ; 救助員	raifugaado ; kyuujo-in

English	Japanese		English	Japanese	
life jacket	ライフジャケット	raifu jakketo	to listen to...	...を聞きます	...o kikimasu (dic. kiku*)
lift (elevator)	エレベーター	erebeetaa	litre	リットル	rittoru
lighter	ライター	raitaa	a little	少し	sukoshi
do you have a lighter?	火（ライター）がありますか	hi (raitaa) ga arimass ka?	to live (in a place)	住みます	sumimasu (dic. sumu*)
light bulb	電球	denkyuu	I live in London	ロンドンに住んでいます	Rondon ni sunde imasu
to like	好きです	suki desu	to be alive	生きています	ikite imasu
I like coffee	コーヒーが好きです	koohii ga suki desu	he is alive	彼は生きています	kare wa ikite imasu
like this	このように；こういう風に	kono yoo ni; kooiu fuu ni	living room	居間	ima
line (railway)	線	sen	lobster	ロブスター	robusutaa
(drawn)	ライン	rain	local	地元	jimoto
list	表；リスト	hyoo; risuto	lock (on door, box)	鍵；ロック	kagi; rokku

English – Japanese

to lock	鍵をかけます	kagi o kakemasu
		(dic. kagi o kakeru*)
locker	ロッカー	rokkaa
long	長い	nagai
for a long time	長い間	nagai aida
to look for	探します	sagashimasu
		(dic. sagasu*)
loose (not fastened)	ゆるい	yurui
to lose	なくします	nakushimasu
		(dic. nakusu*)
I've lost...	...をなくしました	...o nakushimashita
lost (object)	なくした	nakushita
lost property office	紛失物取扱所	funshitsubutsu toriatsukai-sho

a lot	たくさん	takusan
lotion	ローション	rooshon
loud	うるさい	urusai
love (n)	愛	ai
I love swimming	水泳が大好きです	suiei ga daisuki desu
luggage	手荷物	tenimotsu
luggage allowance	手荷物制限	tenimotsu seigen
luggage rack (in car, train)	網棚	amidana
lunch	昼ごはん ; ランチ	hiru gohan ; ranchi
luxury	贅沢 (な)	zeitaku (na)

M

machine	機械	kikai	market	市場 ;	ichiba ; maaketto
				マーケット	
magazine	雑誌	zasshi	marmalade	マーマレード	maamareedo
mail (n)	郵便	yuubin	to marry	結婚します	kekkon shimasu
by mail	郵便で	yuubin de			(dic. kekkon
to make	作ります	tsukurimasu			suru*)
		(dic. tsukuru*)	martial arts	武道	budoo
make-up	(お)化粧	(o-)keshoo	mask	仮面 ; マスク	kamen ; masuku
man (general)	人	hito	mass (in church)	ミサ	misa
(male)	男	otoko	match (game)	試合	shiai
manager	責任者 ;	sekininsha ;	matches	マッチ	matchi
	マネージャー	maneejaa	to matter	気になります	kininarimasu
many	たくさんの	takusan-no			(dic. kininaru*)
map	地図	chizu	it doesn't	構いません	kamaimasen
marathon	マラソン	marason	matter		
March	三月	san-gatsu	mattress	マットレス	mattoresu
			May	五月	go-gatsu

English	Japanese	Romaji
meal	食事	shokuji
to mean	意味します	imishimasu
		(dic. imisuru*)
what does this mean?	これはどういう意味ですか	kore wa doo iu imi desu ka
meat	(お)肉	(o-)niku
mechanic	機械工；メカニック	kikaikoo ; mekanikku
medical insurance	医療保険	iryoo-hoken
medicine	薬	kusuri
medieval	中世の	chuusei-no
to meet	会います	aimasu (dic. au*)
let's meet again	また会いましょう	mata aimashoo
meeting	ミーティング；会議	miitingu ; kaigi

English	Japanese	Romaji
member (of club, etc)	会員；メンバー	kaiin ; menbaa
menu	メニュー	menyuu
message	伝言；メッセージ	dengon ; messeeji
metre	メートル	meetoru
microwave	電子レンジ	denshi renji
midday	お昼	ohiru
at midday	お昼に	ohiru ni
middle-aged	中年の	chuunen-no
midnight	真夜中	mayonaka
migraine	偏頭痛	henzutsuu
milk	ミルク；牛乳	miruku ; gyuunyuu
semi-skimmed	低脂肪牛乳	teishiboo gyuunyuu
soya milk	豆乳	toonyuu

millimetre	ミリメートル	miri-meetoru	monastery	修道院	shuudooin
million (n)	百万	hyaku-man	Monday	月曜日	getsu-yoobi
(adj)	百万の	hyaku-man-no	money	(お)金	(o-)kane
mineral water	ミネラルウォーター	mineraru wootaa	I have no money	お金がありません	okane ga arimasen
minibar	ミニバー	mini baa	month	月	tsuki
minute	分	fun	moon	月	tsuki
one minute	一分	ippun	more	もっと	motto
two minutes	二分	nifun	more wine	もっとワイン	motto wain o
mirror	鏡	kagami	please	をください	kudasai
to miss (train, etc)	乗り遅れます	noriokuremasu (dic. noriokureru*)	no more thank you	もう結構です	moo kekkoo desu
			morning	朝	asa
missing (person)	行方不明	yukuefumei	in the morning	午前中に	gozenchuu ni
mistake	間違い	machigai	this morning	今朝	kesa
mobile phone	携帯電話	keitai denwa	mosquito	蚊	ka
modem	モデム	modemu			

English – Japanese

English – Japanese

mother (own)	母	haha
(somebody else's)	お母さん	okaa-san
motorway	高速道路	koosoku dooro
mountain	山	yama
mountain bike	マウンテンバイク	maunten baiku
mouse (animal)	ねずみ	nezumi
(computer)	マウス	mausu
mouth	口	kuchi
Mr...	...氏; ...さん	...-shi; ...-san
Mrs...	...さん; ...夫人	...-san; ...-fujin
Ms...	...さん	...-san
much	多くの	ookuno
there's too much	多すぎます	oosugimasu
museum	博物館	hakubutsu-kan
mushroom	マッシュルーム	masshuruumu
(Japanese)	しいたけ	shiitake
music	音楽	ongaku
mussel	ムラサキ貝; ムール貝	murasaki-gai; muuru-gai

N

nail (finger)	つめ	tsume
(metal)	釘	kugi
name	名前	namae
what's your name?	お名前は何ですか	o-namae wa nan desu ka?
nappy	オムツ	omutsu
narrow	狭い	semai
nationality	国籍	kokuseki
nausea	吐き気	hakike

English	Japanese		
near	近くに	chikaku-ni	
necessary	必要（な）	hitsuyoo(na)	
neck	首	kubi	
necklace	ネックレス	nekkuresu	
to need	必要です	hitsuyoo desu	
I need...	...が必要です	...ga hitsuyoo	
		desu	
needle	針	hari	
negative (photograph)	ネガ	nega	
neighbour	近所	kinjo	
nephew	甥	oi	
never (adv)	絶対...ません	zettai...masen	
I never drink wine	絶対ワインを飲みません	zettai wain o nomimasen	
new	新しい	atarashii	

English	Japanese		
news	ニュース；知らせ	nyuusu:.. (o-)shirase	
newspaper	新聞	shimbun	
New Year	新年	shinnen	
New Zealand	ニュージーランド	nyuujiirando	
New Zealander (person)	ニュージーランド人	nyuujiirando-jin	
next	次	tsugi	
next week	来週	raishuu	
next year	来年	rainen	
the next train	次の電車	tsugi no densha	
night	夜	yoru	
at night	夜に	yoru ni	
last night	昨夜；夕べ	sakuya:yuube	
tomorrow night	明日の夜	ashita no yoru	

English – Japanese

English – Japanese

nightclub	ナイトクラブ	naito kurabu	now	今	ima
nightdress	寝巻き	nemaki	nowadays	このごろ	konogoro
no	いいえ	iie	number (of)	数	kazu
no, thank you	結構です	kekoo desu	number	数字	suuji
noisy	うるさい	urusai	(1, 2, 3, etc.)		
non-alcoholic	アルコール抜き	arukooru nuki	nurse	看護師	kangoshi
			O		
non-smoking	禁煙	kin-en	object (thing)	物	mono
non-smoking compartment	禁煙車両	kinen sharyoo	October	十月	juu-gatsu
			octopus	たこ	tako
noodles	麺	men	of (possessive)	...の	...no
north	北	kita	off (light)	消えています	kiete imasu
Northern Ireland	北アイルランド	Kita Airurando			(dic. kiete iru*)
note (banknote)	紙幣	shihei	(food)	腐っています	kusatte imasu
(letter)	メモ	memo			(dic. kusatte iru*)
November	十一月	juuichi-gatsu			

English		Japanese	
office	オフィス；事務所	ofisu ; jimusho
often	よく	yoku
oil	油	abura
oil filter	オイルフィルター	oiru firutaa
OK	オーケー	ookei
I'm ok, it's ok	大丈夫です	daijoobu desu
ok, let's do that	オーケー、そうしましょう	ookei, soo shimashoo
old (adj)	古い	furui
how old are you?	おいくつですか	oikutsu desu ka?
olive	オリーブ	oriibu
omelette	オムレツ	omuretsu
on (light)	ついています	tsuite imasu
		(dic. tsuite iru*)
on the table	テーブルの上に	teeburu no ue ni
one (adj)	ひとつの	hitotsu-no
(n)	一	ichi
one-way ticket	片道切符	katamichi kippu
onion	たまねぎ	tamanegi
to open	開けます	akemasu
		(dic. akeru*)
the shop is open	営業中です	eigyoo-chuu desu
the door is open	ドアが開いています	doa ga aite imasu
operation (medical)	手術	shujutsu
opposite	反対	hantai
optician	メガネ店	megane-ten

English – Japanese

English – Japanese

orange (colour)	オレンジ色	orenji-iro		
(fruit)	オレンジ	orenji		
orange juice	オレンジジュース	orenjijuusu		
out	外	soto		
out of order	故障中	koshoo-chuu		
he's out	彼は外出中です	kare wa gaishutsu-chuu desu		
outdoor (pool, etc.)	野外	yagai		
oven	オーブン	oobun		
overnight train	夜行列車	yakoo ressha		
oysters	牡蠣	kaki		

P

Pacific Ocean	太平洋	taiheiyoo
packet	小包	kozutsumi
painful	痛い	itai
painkiller	鎮痛剤	chintsuuzai
painting	絵	e
(oil) painting	油絵	abura-e
palace	宮殿	kyuuden
pants (trousers)	ズボン	zubon
pants (men's underwear)	パンツ	pantsu
paper	紙	kami
paper	ティッシュ	tisshu
handkerchief		
paper towels	キッチンペーパー	kitchin peepaa
pardon?	すみません	sumimasen

English	Japanese	
I beg your pardon! (didn't hear/understand)	すみません！／もう一度お願いいします	sumimasen! moo ichido onegai shimasu
parents	両親	ryooshin
your parents	ご両親	go-ryooshin
park (garden)	公園	kooen
parking lot	駐車場	chuusha-joo
partner (wife, husband)	配偶者	haiguusha
party (evening)	パーティー	paatii
(group)	一行；一団	ikkoo: ichidan
pass (permit)	許可証	kyokashoo
passenger	乗客	jookyaku
passport	パスポート	pasupooto
passport control	出入国管理所	shutsunyuukoku kanri-sho
path	小道	komichi
to pay	払います	haraimasu (dic. harau*)
payment	支払い	shiharai
payphone	公衆電話	kooshuu denwa
pear (Japanese)	梨	nashi
pear (western)	洋ナシ	yoonashi
pearl	真珠	shinju
pedestrian (n)	歩行者	hokoosha
pedestrian crossing	横断歩道	oodan-hodoo
pen	ペン	pen
pencil	鉛筆	enpitsu
penicillin	ペニシリン	penishirin
pensioner	年金受給者	nenkin-jukyuu-sha
people	人々	hitobito

English – Japanese

English – Japanese

pepper (spice)	コショウ	koshoo
(vegetable)	ピーマン	piiman
per...	...につき	...ni tsuki
per hour	一時間につき	ichi-jikan ni tsuki
per person	一人につき	hitori ni tsuki
percent	パーセント	paasento
perfume	香水	koosui
period (menstruation)	生理	seiri
person	人	hito
personal organizer	電子手帳	denshi techoo
petrol	ガソリン	gasorin
petrol station	ガソリンスタンド	gasorin stando
pharmacy	薬局	yakkyoku
phone (n)	電話	denwa

to phone	電話をかけます	denwa o kakemasu (dic. denwa o kakeru*)
phone box	電話ボックス	denwa bokkusu
phonecard	テレホンカード	terehon kaado
phone number	電話番号	denwa-bangoo
photocopy (n)	コピー	kopii
to photocopy	コピーをします	kopii o shimasu (dic. kopii o suru*)
photograph (n)	写真	shashin
to photograph	写真を撮ります	shashin o torimasu (dic. shashin o toru*)
pig	豚	buta

English	Japanese	
pillow	枕	makura
pineapple	パイナップル	painappuru
plan (of a building)	図面	zumen
to plan	企画します	kikaku shimasu (dic. kikaku suru*)
plane (aircraft)	飛行機	hikooki
plaster (sticking plaster)	バンドエイド	bando-eido
plastic bag	ポリ袋	pori-bukuro
platform (railway)	ホーム	hoomu
play (theatre)	劇	geki
plug (electrical)	プラグ；差込	puragu; sashikomi
plug socket	コンセント	konsento

English	Japanese	
plum (Japanese, green)	梅	ume
plum (western, purple)	プラム	puramu
plumber	配管工；水道屋	haikankoo; suidooya
p.m. (after noon)	午後	gogo
poisonous	有毒な	yuudoku-na
police	警察	keisatsu
policeman	警察官	keesatsu-kan
police station	交番	kooban
pool (swimming)	プール	puuru
pork	豚肉	buta-niku
portion (of food)	一人前	ichinin-mae
postcard	絵葉書	e-hagaki
post code	郵便番号	yuubin bangoo
post office	郵便局	yuubinkyoku
pound	ポンド	pondo

English – Japanese

English – Japanese

power cut	停電	teiden	
power point	コンセント	konsento	
prawn	海老	ebi	
pregnant	妊娠	ninshin	
prescription	処方箋	shohoosen	
present/gift	贈り物 ; プレゼント	okurimono ; purezento	
president (of a company)	社長	shachoo	
pretty	かわいい	kawaii	
price	値段	nedan	
priest (Buddhist)	僧侶	sooryo	
(Catholic)	神父	shimpu	
(Protestant)	牧師	bokushi	
prince	王子	ooji	
princess	王女	oojo	
private	個人の	kojin-no	

prize	賞品	shoohin	
problem	問題	mondai	
there's a *problem*	問題があります	mondai ga arimasu	
programme (TV, etc.)	番組	bangumi	
(computer)	プログラム	puroguramu	
promise	約束	yakusoku	
it's a promise	約束です	yakusoku desu	
to pronounce	発音します	hatsuon shimasu	
		(dic. hatsuon suru*)	
how is it *pronounced?*	どのように発音しますか	donoyooni hatsuon shimasu ka?	
Protestant	新教徒	shinkyooto	
public holiday	祭日	saijitsu	

English	Japanese		
public toilet	公衆トイレ	kooshuu toire	
to pull	引きます	hikimasu	
		(dic. hiku*)	
puncture	パンク	panku	
purse	財布	saifu	
to push	押します	oshimasu	
		(dic. osu*)	
pushchair	バギー ; ベビーカー	bagii ; bebiikaa	

Q

qualification	資格	shikaku
quality	品質	hinshitsu
queen	女王	joooo
question (n)	質問	shitsumon
queue	列	retsu
quickly	速く	hayaku

quiet (place)	静かな	shizuka-na

R

rabies	狂犬病	kyookenbyoo
race (sport)	競走	kyoosoo
(people)	人種	jinshu
radio	ラジオ	rajio
railway station	駅	eki
rain	雨	ame
it's raining	雨が降っています	ame ga futte imasu
rare (unique)	まれ	mare
(food)	レアー	reaa
rash (skin)	発疹	hasshin
raw	生	nama
razor	かみそり	kamisori
razor blades	かみそりの刃	kamisori no ha

English – Japanese

English – Japanese

ready	準備	jumbi	
receipt	領収書；	ryooshuusho ;	
	レシート	reshiito	
reception (desk)	受付	uketsuke	
receptionist	受付係	uketsuke-gakari	
recipe	レシピ；	reshipi ;	
	調理法	choorihoo	
to recommend	薦めます	susumemasu	
		(dic. susumeru*)	
what do you recommend?	何がお薦めですか	nani ga osusume desu ka	
record (music)	レコード	rekoodo	
red (n)	赤	aka	
(adj)	赤い	akai	
reduction (for students, etc.)	割引	waribiki	
refreshments	軽食	keishoku	

refund	返金	henkin	
I'd like a refund	返金してください	henkin shite kudasai	
region	地域；地方	chiiki ; chihoo	
to reimburse	返済します	hensai shimasu (dic. hensai suru*)	
relative (family member)	親戚	shinseki	
relatively (comparatively)	比較的	hikakuteki	
reliable (person)	信頼できる	shinrai dekiru	
religion	宗教	shuukyoo	
to rent	借ります	karimasu (dic. kariru*)	
rent (for house, flat)	家賃	yachin	

English	Japanese		
to repair	修理します ； 直します	shuuri shimasu (dic. shuuri suru*); naoshimasu (dic. naosu*)	restaurant car	食堂車	shokudoosha
to repeat	繰り返します	kurikaeshimasu (dic. kurikaesu*)	retire	引退します	intai shimasu (dic. intai suru*)
can you repeat that, please?	もう一度言って ください	moo ichido itte kudasai	to return (to go back)	帰ります ； 戻ります	kaerimasu (dic. kaeru*); modorimasu (dic. modoru*)
reservation	予約	yoyaku	(to give back)	返します	kaeshimasu (dic. kaesu*)
reserved seat	指定席	shitei-seki	(to return a purchase)	返品します	hempin shimasu (dic. hempin suru*)
resort (seaside)	リゾート	rizooto	return ticket	往復切符	oofuku-kippu
rest (relaxation)	休息	kyuusoku	reverse-charge call (collect call)	コレクトコール	korekuto kooru
to rest	休息します	kyuusoku shimasu (dic. kyuusoku suru*)	rheumatism	リュウマチ	ryuumachi
restaurant	レストラン	resutoran			

English - Japanese

English – Japanese

English	Japanese	Romaji
rice (cooked)	(お)米 ご飯	(o-)kome gohan
right (correct)	正しい	tadashii
on/to the right	右に	migi ni
ring (for finger)	指輪	yubiwa
river	川	kawa
road	道；道路	michi ; dooro
road sign	道路標識	dooro hyooshiki
to roast, bake or grill	焼きます	yakimasu
	(dic. yaku*)	
room (in house, hotel)	部屋	heya
(space)	場所	basho
it takes up	場所をとります	basho o torimasu
room service	ルームサービス	ruumu saabisu

English	Japanese	Romaji
rotten (meat, fruit)	腐った	kusatta
route	ルート；順路	ruuto ; junro
row (theatre, etc.)	列	retsu
royal	王室の	ooshitsu-no
rubbish (nonsense)	ごみ	gomi
	たわごと	tawagoto
rucksack	リュックサック	ryukkusakku
rush hour	ラッシュ	rasshu

S

safe (adj)	安全な	anzen-na
safety belt	安全ベルト	anzen beruto
sailing (sport)	セーリング	seeringu
salad	サラダ	sarada

English	Japanese		English	Japanese	
salary	サラリー； 給料	sararii ; kyuuryoo	to save (life)	救います	sukuimasu (dic. sukuu*)
sale (in shops)	セール	seeru	to save	蓄えます ；	takuwaemasu
salesman	セールスマン	seerusuman	(money)	貯金します	(dic. takuwaeru*); chokin shimasu
(in store)	店員	ten-in			(dic. chokin suru*)
salmon	鮭	sake	to say	言います	iimasu (dic. iu*)
salt	塩	shio	scales (for	はかり	hakari
sandals	サンダル	sandaru	weighing)		
sandwich	サンドイッチ	sandoitchi	scenery	景色	keshiki
sanitary towel	整理用ナプキン	seiriyoo napukin	school	学校	gakkoo
			scissors	はさみ	hasami
sardine	鰯	iwashi	Scotland	スコットラン ド	Sukottorando
satellite channels	衛星放送	eisei hoosoo	Scottish (adj)	スコットラン ドの	Sukottorando-no
Saturday	土曜日	do-yoobi	screw (n)	ねじ	neji
sauce	ソース	soosu			

English – Japanese

English – Japanese

English	Japanese	romaji
screwdriver	ドライバー	doraibaa
scuba diving	スキューバダイビング	sukyuuba daibingu
sculpture (object)	彫刻	chookoku
sea	海	umi
seafood	シーフード；海鮮料理	shiifuudo ; kaisen-ryoori
seasickness	船酔い	funayoi
seaside	海辺	umibe
at the seaside	海辺で	umibe de
season (of year)	季節	kisetsu
season ticket	定期券	teiki-ken
seat	席	seki
seatbelt	シートベルト	shiitoberuto
seaweed	海草	kaisoo
secretary	秘書	hisho
security guard	警備員	keibi-in
to see	見ます	mimasu (dic. miru*)
self-catering	自炊	jisui
self-service	セルフサービス	serufu saabisu
to sell	売ります	urimasu (dic. uru*)
Sellotape®	セロテープ	seroteepu
to send	送ります	okurimasu (dic. okuru*)
to send someone off	見送ります	miokurimasu (dic. miokuru*)
senior citizen	高齢者	koorei-sha
September	九月	ku-gatsu
service (in restaurant, etc.)	サービス	saabisu

service charge	サービス料	saabisuryoo
set menu	定食	teishoku
sex	性別	seibetsu
shampoo	シャンプー	shampuu
to share	分担します；分けます	buntan shimasu (dic. buntan suru*); wakemasu (dic. wakeru*)
shares (stocks)	株	kabu
to shave	そります	sorimasu (dic. soru*)
shaving cream	髭剃りのクリーム	higesori kuriimu
sheet	シーツ	shitsu
shellfish	魚介類	gyokairui
ship	船	fune

shirt	シャツ	shatsu
shoe	靴	kutsu
shoe polish	靴磨き	kutsu-migaki
shop	店	mise
shopping	買い物	kaimono
to go shopping	買い物します	kaimono shimasu (dic. kaimono suru*)
shopping trolley	ショッピングカート	shoppingu kaato
short cut	近道	chikamichi
shorts	半ズボン	hanzubon
shoulder	肩	kata
show (at theatre, etc.)	ショー	shoo
shower	シャワー	shawaa
shrimps	小エビ	ko-ebi

English – Japanese

shrine	神社	jinja
to shut	閉めます	shimemasu (dic. shimeru*)
sick (ill)	病気	byooki
to be sick (vomit)	吐きます	hakimasu (dic. haku*)
sightseeing	観光	kankoo
signature	署名；サイン	shomei; sain
silk	絹	kinu
silver (n)	銀	gin
silver (adj)	銀の	gin-no
single (person)	独身	dokushin
single (bed, room)	一人用	hitoriyoo
single (ticket)	片道	katamichi
sink (bathroom etc.)	流し；洗面台	nagashi; senmendai

sisters	姉妹	shimai
sister (own, younger)	妹	imooto
sister (own, older)	姉	ane
sister (somebody else's, younger)	妹さん	imooto-san
sister (somebody else's, older)	お姉さん	onee-san
size	大きさ	ookisa
size (clothes)	サイズ	saizu
to ski	スキーをします	skii o shimasu (dic. sukii o suru*)
ski boots	スキー靴	skii-gutsu
ski pass	リフト券	lifuto ken
skirt	スカート	sukaato

English					
to sleep	寝ます	nemasu	soap	石鹸	sekken
	(dic. neru*)		soap powder	粉石鹸	kona sekken
sleeping bag	寝袋	nebukuro	sober (not drunk)	素面	shirafu
sleeping pill	睡眠薬	suiminyaku	sock	靴下	kutsushita
slippers	スリッパ	surippa	soda water	炭酸水	tansan sui
slow	遅い	osoi	soft drink	ソフトドリン	sofuto dorinku
small	小さい	chiisai		ク	
smell (n)	におい	nioi	something	何か	nani ka
to smoke	タバコをすいます	tabako o suimasu	sometimes	時々	tokidoki
	(dic. tabako o suu*)		son (own)	息子	musuko
smoking	喫煙	kitsuen	son (somebody else's)	息子さん	musuko-san
no smoking	禁煙	kinen	song	歌	uta
snack	軽食	keishoku	soon	すぐ	sugu
snow (n)	雪	yuki	sore head	頭痛	zutsuu
it's snowing	雪が降っています	yuki ga futte imasu	sore throat	のどの痛み	nodo no itami
			sorry	すみません	sumimasen
			I'm sorry	すみません	sumimasen

English – Japanese

English	Japanese (kana/kanji)	Romaji
soup	スープ	suupu
south	南	minami
South Africa	南アフリカ	Minami Afurika
South African (person)	南アフリカ人	Minami Afurika-jin
souvenir	お土産 ; 記念品	o-miyage ; kinen-hin
soy sauce	醤油	shooyu
spanner	レンチ	renchi
to speak	話します	hanashimasu (dic. hanasu*)
do you speak English?	英語が話せますか？	Eigo ga hanasemasu ka?
speciality	専門	semmon
speed limit	制限速度	seigen sokudo
to spell	綴ります	tsuaurimasu (dic. tsuzuru*)
how is it spelt?	綴りを教えてください	tsuzuri o oshiete kudasai
to spend (money)	（お金を）使います	(okane o) tsukaimasu (dic. tsukau*)
spicy	辛い	karai
spirits (alcohol)	蒸留酒	jooryuushu
spoon	スプーン	supuun
sport	スポーツ	supootsu
sprain (ankle, etc.)	捻挫	nenza
spring (season)	春	haru
hot spring (water)	温泉	onsen
squash (game, drink)	スカッシュ	sukasshu
squid	イカ	ika

English		
stadium	スタジアム；競技場	sutajiamu; kyoogijoo
stamps (for letters)	切手	kitte
star (in sky)	星	hoshi
star (film)	スター	sutaa
station	駅	eki
stationer's	文房具屋	bunboogu-ya
statue	像	zoo
steak	ステーキ	steeki
steep	険しい	kewashii
stereo	ステレオ	stereo
sting (n)	刺し傷	sashi-kizu
stomach	おなか	onaka
stomach ache	腹痛	fukutsuu
storm	嵐	arashi
straight on	まっすぐ	massugu
strange (odd)	変な	hen-na
strawberry	イチゴ	ichigo
street	通り	toori
string (for wrapping)	紐	himo
strong (person)	強い	tsuyoi
strong (material)	丈夫な	joobu-na
stuck (jammed)	詰まっている	tsumatte iru
student	学生	gakusei
suburbs	郊外	koogai
subway (metro)	地下鉄	chikatetsu
suddenly	突然	totsuzen
sugar	砂糖	satoo
sugar-free	無糖	mutoo
suit	スーツ	suutsu
suitcase	スーツケース	suutsu keesu
summer	夏	natsu

English – Japanese

English – Japanese

English	Japanese	romaji			
sun	太陽	taiyoo	sweetener	甘味料	kanmiryoo
to sunbathe	日光浴をします	nikkooyoku o shimasu (dic. nikkooyoku o suru*)	sweets	お菓子	o-kashi
			to swim	泳ぎます	oyogimasu (dic. oyogu*)
suntan	日焼け	hiyake	swimsuit	水着	mizugi
Sunday	日曜日	nichi-yoobi	to switch off	切ります	kirimasu (dic. kiru*)
sunglasses	サングラス	sangurasu	to switch on	入れます	iremasu (dic. ireru*)
sunscreen	日焼け止め	hiyake-dome	synagogue	ユダヤ教会堂	yudaya-kyookaidoo
sunstroke	日射病	nisshabyoo			
supermarket	スーパー	suupaa	**T**		
supper (dinner)	夕食	yuushoku	table	テーブル	teeburu
surgery (of doctor)	診察室	shinsatsu-shitsu	to take	かかります	kakarimasu (dic. kakaru*)
surname	苗字	myooji			
sweet (not savoury)	甘い	amai			

English	Japanese	Romaji
how long does it take?	どのぐらいか かかりますか	dono gurai kakarimasu ka?
to talk	話します	hanashimasu (dic. hanasu*)
tampon	タンポン	tampon
tangerines	みかん	mikan
tap	蛇口	jaguchi
tape (sticky)	粘着テープ	nenchaku teepu
tape (audio)	カセットテープ	kasetto teepu
to taste (of something)	味わいます	ajiwaimasu (dic. ajiwau*)
to taste (something)	食べてみます	tabetemimasu (dic. tabetemiru*)
tax	税金	zeikin
tax-free	免税	menzei
taxi	タクシー	takushii
by taxi	タクシーで	takushii de
taxi driver	タクシーの運転手	takushii no untenshu
taxi rank	タクシー乗り場	takushii noriba
tea (green)	お茶	o-cha
(English)	紅茶	koocha
teacher	先生	sensei
teeth	歯	ha
telephone (n)	電話	denwa
telephone box	電話ボックス	denwa bokkusu
telephone directory	電話帳	denwa choo
telephone number	電話番号	denwa bangoo
television	テレビ	terebi

English	Japanese		English	Japanese	
to tell	言います	iimasu (dic. iu*)	that one (near the listener)	それ	sore
temperature	熱	netsu	(away from the listener and speaker)	あれ	are
I have a temperature	熱があります	netsu ga arimasu			
temple	(お)寺	(o-)tera	theatre	劇場	gekijoo
tennis	テニス	tenisu	thermometer	温度計	ondokei
tennis court	テニスコート	tenisu kooto	thick (paper, board)	厚い	atsui
tennis racket	テニスラケット	tenisu raketto	(rope, cord)	太い	futoi
			(sauce)	濃い	koi
tent	テント	tento	thief	泥棒	doroboo
terminal (airport)	ターミナル	taaminaru	thin (paper, sauce)	薄い	usui
			(rope, cord)	細い	hosoi
thank you	ありがとう	arigatoo	thing	物	mono
thank you	(どうも)ありがとう	(doomo) arigatoo	my things	私のもの	watashi no mono
very much	ありがとう ございます	gozaimasu			

thirsty	のどが渇きます	nodo ga kawakimasu
		(dic. nodo ga kawaku*)
I'm thirsty	のどが渇きました	nodo ga kawakimashita
this one	これ	kore
throat	のど	nodo
thunder	雷	kaminari
thunderstorm	雷雨	raiu
Thursday	木曜日	moku-yoobi
ticket	切符；チケット	kippu ; chiketto
ticket office	切符売り場	kippu uriba
ticket vending machine	切符販売機	kippu hanbai-ki
tight	きつい	kitsui

tights	タイツ	taitsu
time	時間	jikan
this time	今回	konkai
what time is it?	何時ですか	nan-ji desu ka?
timetable (train, etc.)	スケジュール	sukejuuru
	時刻表	jikoku-hyoo
tinned	缶詰	kanzume
tinfoil	アルミホイル	arumi hoiru
tin-opener	缶きり	kankiri
tired	疲れます	tsukaremasu
		(dic. tsukareru*)
I'm tired	疲れました	tsukaremashita
tissue	ティッシュ	tisshu
toast (bread)	トースト	toosuto
tobacconist's	タバコ屋	tabako-ya
today	今日	kyoo

English – Japanese

English	Japanese	romaji
toilet (informal)	トイレ	toire
(polite)	お手洗い	o-tearai
toilet paper	トイレット	toiretto peepaa
	ペーパー	
toiletries	化粧品	keshoohin
toll (motorway)	通行料	tsuukooryoo
tomato	トマト	tomato
tomorrow	明日	ashita
tomorrow	明日の朝	ashita no asa
morning		
tomorrow	明日の午後	ashita no gogo
afternoon		
tomorrow	明日の夜	ashita no yoru
night		
tonight	今夜；今晩	konya ; konban
tooth	歯	ha
toothache	歯痛	haita

English	Japanese	romaji
toothbrush	歯ブラシ	haburashi
toothpaste	歯磨き粉	hamigakiko
torch	懐中電灯	kaichuu-dentoo
tough (meat)	かたい	katai
tour (sightseeing)	ツアー	tsuaa
tourist	観光客	kankoo-kyaku
tourist office	観光案内所	kankoo-annai-sho
towel	タオル	taoru
town	町	machi
town centre	町の中心	machi no chuushin
town plan	都市計画	toshi-keikaku
toy	おもちゃ	omocha
tracksuit	トレーニング	toreeningu ueaa
	ウェアー	
tradition	伝統	dentoo

traffic	交通	kootsuu
traffic jam	交通渋滞	kootsuu-juutai
traffic lights	信号	shingoo
train	電車	densha
translation	翻訳	honyaku
translator	翻訳家	honyaku-ka
to travel	旅行します	ryokoo shimasu
		(dic. ryoko suru*)
travel agent's	旅行代理店	ryokoo dairiten
traveller's	トラベラーズ	toraberaazu
cheque	チェック	chekku
tree	木	ki
trip	旅行	ryokoo
trousers	ズボン	zubon
trout	ます	masu
true (real)	本当	hontoo

Tuesday	火曜日	ka-yoobi
tuna	マグロ	maguro
to turn off	消します	keshimasu
(light, etc.)		(dic. kesu*)
to turn on	つけます	tsukemasu
(light, etc.)		(dic. tsukeru*)
tweezers	毛抜き	kenuki
twin-bed room	ツインベッド	tsuinbeddo no
	の部屋	heya
tyre	タイヤ	taiya

U

ulcer	潰瘍	kaiyoo
umbrella	かさ	kasa
uncle (own)	おじ	oji
(somebody else's)	おじさん	oji-san

underground (metro)	地下鉄	chikatetsu
to understand	わかります	wakarimasu (dic. wakaru*)
I don't understand	わかりません	wakarimasen
do you understand?	わかりますか	wakarimasu ka
underwear	下着	shitagi
unemployed	無職	mushoku
United Kingdom	英国；イギリス	Eikoku；Igirisu
United States of America	アメリカ合衆国	Amerika Gasshuukoku
university	大学	daigaku
unpack (case)	荷解き	nihodoki
urgent	緊急	kinkyuu

V

vacancy (in hotel)	空き室	akishitsu
vaccination	予防注射	yoboo-chuusha
valid (passport, etc.)	有効な	yuukoo-na
valuables	貴重品	kichoo-hin
van	パン；ワゴン車	ban；wagon-sha
vase	花瓶	kabin
VAT	付加価値税	fukakachi-zei
vegetable	野菜	yasai
vegetarian	ベジタリアン；菜食主義者	bejitarian；saishoku-shugi-sha
vehicle	乗り物	norimono
very	大変；とても	taihen；totemo
video	ビデオ	bideo

video game	ビデオゲーム	bideo geemu	waiting room	待合室	machiai-shitsu
village	村	mura	waitress	ウエイトレス	ueitoresu
vinegar	酢	su	to wake up	起きます	okimasu
virus	ウイルス	uirus			(dic. okiru*)
visa	ビザ	biza	Wales	ウエールズ	Ueeruzu
to visit	たずねます	tazunemasu	to walk	歩きます	arukimasu
		(dic. tazuneru*)			(dic. aruku*)
visitor	客	kyaku	to go for	散歩します	sampo shimasu
(tourist)	観光客	kankoo-kyaku	a walk		(dic. sampo
vitamin	ビタミン	bitamin			suru*)
			wallet	財布	saifu
W			to want	欲しいです	hoshii desu
wage	賃金；給料	chingin, kyuuryo	wardrobe	洋服ダンス	yoofuku-dansu
waist	ウエスト	uesuto	warm	暖かい	atatakai
to wait for...	…を待ちます	...o machimasu	to wash	洗います	araimasu
		(dic. matsu*)			(dic. arau*)
waiter	ウエイター	ueitaa			

248 | 249

English – Japanese

English – Japanese

English	Japanese	Reading
washing machine	洗濯機	sentaku-ki
washing-up liquid	液体洗剤	ekitai-senzai
washing powder	粉石けん	kona-sekken
wasp	スズメバチ	suzumebachi
watch (on wrist)	腕時計	udedokei
to watch TV	テレビを見ます	terebi o mimasu (dic. miru*)
water	水	mizu
hot water	お湯	oyu
water heater	湯沸かし器	yuwakashiki
watermelon	すいか	suika
waterproof	防水	boosui
water-skiing	水上スキー	suijoo-skii
way (manner)	仕方	shikata
(route)	方向	hookoo
way in	入口	iriguchi
way out	出口	deguchi
we	私たち	watashi-tachi
weak (physically)	弱い	yowai
(tea, etc.)	うすい	usui
weather	天気	tenki
weather forecast	天気予報	tenki yohoo
website	ウェブサイト	uebu saito
wedding	結婚式	kekkon-shiki
Wednesday	水曜日	sui-yoobi
week	週	shuu
weekday	平日	heijitsu
weekend	週末	shuumatsu
weekly	毎週	maishuu

English	Japanese		English	Japanese	
weight	重さ	omosa			
well	よい	yoi			
well done	よくできました	yoku dekimashita	*which is it?*	どれですか	dore desu ka
			whisky	ウイスキー	uisukii
I am well	元気です	genki desu	*white* (n)	白	shiro
Welsh (person)	ウェールズ人	ueeruzu-jin	(adj)	白い	shiroi
west (n)	西	nishi	who	誰	dare
(adj)	西の	nishi-no	whose	誰の	dareno
wet	ぬれた	nureta	*whose is it?*	誰のですか	dareno desu ka
what	何	nani; nan	why	なぜ；	naze ; dooshite
what is it?	それは何です	sore wa nan desu		どうして	
	か	ka	wide	広い	hiroi
			widow	未亡人	miboojin
wheel (of car)	車輪	sharin	wife (own)	妻	tsuma
wheelchair	車椅子	kuruma-isu	(somebody else's)	奥さん	oku-san
when	いつ	itsu	to win	勝ちます	kachimasu
where	どこ	doko			(dic. katsu*)
which	どれ；どちら	dore ; dochira	wind (air)	風	kaze
			window	窓	mado

English – Japanese

English – Japanese

windscreen	フロントガラス	furonto garasu	
windscreen wipers	ワイパー	waipaa	
windsurfing	ウィンドサーフィン	uindo saafin	
wine	ワイン	wain	
red wine	赤ワイン	aka wain	
white wine	白ワイン	shiro wain	
wine list	ワインリスト	wain risuto	
winter	冬	fuyu	
with (a person)	…と一緒に	…to issho ni	
woman	女	onna	
wonderful	すばらしい	subarashii	
wood	木；ウール	ki	
wool	毛；ウール	ke；uuru	
word	単語	tango	

to work (person)	働きます	hatarakimasu (dic. hataraku*)	
(machine, car)	動きます	ugokimasu (dic. ugoku*)	
world	世界	sekai	
wrist	手首	tekubi	
to write	書きます	kakimasu (dic. kaku*)	
writer (author)	著者	chosha	
wrong	悪い	warui	
X			
x-ray	レントゲン	rentogen	

Y		
year	年	nen ; toshi
for one year	一年間	ichi-nen-kan
one year old	一歳	issai
five years old	五歳	go-sai
next year	来年	rainen
last year	去年	kyonen
yellow (n)	黄色	kiiro
(adj)	黄色い	kiiroi
yes	はい	hai
yes please	はい、お願いします	hai, onegai shimasu
yesterday	昨日	kinoo
yet	まだ	mada
not yet	まだです	mada desu
youth hostel	ユースホステル	yuusu hosuteru

Z		
zebra crossing	横断歩道	oodan hodoo
zero	ゼロ；零	zero ; rei
zip	チャック；ファスナー	chakku ; fasunaa
zone	ゾーン；地帯	zoon ; chitai
zoo	動物園	doobutsu-en

*You must use this form when you look up a word in a conventional dictionary.

English – Japanese

Further titles in Collins' phrasebook range
Collins Gem Phrasebook

Also available as **Phrasebook CD Pack**
Other titles in the series

Arabic	Greek	Polish
Cantonese	Italian	Portuguese
Croatian	Japanese	Russian
Czech	Korean	Spanish
Dutch	Latin American	Thai
French	Spanish	Turkish
German	Mandarin	Vietnamese

Collins Phrasebook & Dictionary

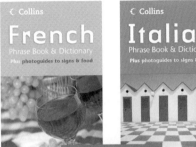

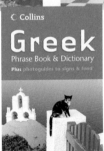

Also available as **Phrasebook CD Pack**
Other titles in the series
German Japanese Portuguese Spanish

Collins Easy: Photo Phrasebook

Also available as
**Phrasebook
CD Pack**

**Other titles
in the series**
Easy French
Easy Greek
Easy Italian

To order any of these titles, please telephone
0870 787 1732. For further information about all
Collins books, visit our website: www.collins.co.uk